MW00377975

Natural Health Care
For Your Four-Legged Friends
Using Essential Oils and
Supplements

Second Edition

Sara Kenney

Helping people & pet owners
choose a natural, healthy
lifestyle using aromatherapy.

www.aromateam.net

Legal Information

Disclaimer of Liability

The author and publishers shall have neither liability nor responsibility to any person(s) or entities with respect to any loss or damage, caused or alleged to be caused directly or indirectly as a result of the information contained in this book, or appearing on The Aroma Team website. While this book is as accurate as the author can make it, there may be unintentional errors, omissions and inaccuracies.

Terms and Conditions

This book is for informational and educational purposes only. The information presented and contained within this book is based on the training and experience of the author. It's content is not intended to be used as a substitute for veterinary care.

Helping people & pet owners
choose a natural, healthy
lifestyle using aromatherapy.

Contents

Acknowledgements …………………………………………… 6

Preface ………………………………………………… 8

Main Parts of the Horse …………………………………….. 9

Main Parts of the Dog ……………………………………. 10

Main Parts of the Cat …………………………………….. 11

Using a Pendulum ……………………………………….. 13

Section One: Dogs ……………………………………….. 17

Dog Food ………………………………………………. 19

Acupressure for Dogs …………………………………… 49

Section Two: Cats ……………………………………….. 51

Cat Food ………………………………………………. 53

Section Three: Horses ……………………………………. 62

Raindrop Technique ……………………………………. 85

Diffusing Oils and Animals …………………………………. 90

Dog & Cat Emergency Bucket …………………………….. 93

Equine Emergency Bucket ………………………………. 94

Canine Essential Oil Application …………………………… 96

Cat Essential Oil Application ……………………………… 97

Horse Essential Oil Application …………………………… 98

About the Author ………………………………………. 99

Index ………………………………………………….. 100

Acknowledgements

I wish to thank all the animals that were so trusting and patient with me as we journeyed together on this new frontier of using essential oils and supplements in bettering their health. I assure you none were harmed in the making of this book!

To my parents, who sparked the fire for my love of animals and my interest in natural remedies. Who knew that the dog-grooming lesson at age twelve would turn into a 20 year career? The covert trips to the humane society "Just to look, mom" and rarely coming home without something that needed us, was just training for the future. Dad your interest in natural remedies… well I was listening and you didn't mind when the student became the teacher. Thank you both for fanning that flame and being so supportive.

Most importantly, I have to thank my husband Rodger for having the fortitude to put up with all the adventurous paths I've led us down! He never knows what he'll find when he comes home… I've had a horse take over his garage, he did quite a job licking all the windows of the car!

I have had anywhere from 1 to 25 boarding dogs as well as numerous boarding cats downstairs in our house, and up to 35 dogs in the backyard kennels. Not to mention coming home to find I had moved an elk calf into the basement one day. Animal control brought it to me hoping I could help. He was with us a couple weeks for malnourishment and recuperation. There was a fawn as well.

Of course I added miniature horses to our menagerie and my patient husband would just shake his head as i slept for many nights in a row, outside in a three-sided shed awaiting the birth of foals. This is March and April, in Montana, snow, sleet, hail and rain could not make me leave that shed until a healthy foal was up and about. He would check on us periodically, with a hot chocolate in hand for me, and be on child watch in the house through the night for our kids. Yes, he's a patient man.

A thank you to our kids who grew up helping with boarding chores, greeting customers and grabbing oils and the supply bucket then running to me with them when emergencies struck!

It has been a pleasure, over the years, to work with animals and share my experiences with others, giving them the interest and confidence to use them too. I thank my niece, Mindy Schroder. She was with me in the filming of Essential Tips for Happy Healthy Pets, sharing her horse Abby for the filming and she continues to share her animals with me on my projects. A special thanks to Destino, her beautiful Andalusian gelding, Gentry, her regal Standard Poodle and Mr. Firefly, the mighty miniature horse, as well as the other wonderful horses, dogs and cats that appear in this book.

A very special thanks to Mindy also as, without her, this book would still be an unfinished plan, a handmade workbook. Her expertise, time, diligence and her photography have brought it to fruition at last.

Thank you to my sister, Loree and her Italian Mastiff, Bella. Bella, your paws are big enough to let people see right where to put the oils!

I appreciate all who wanted to share testimonials in this book. We picked a few that we thought would be most helpful. I thank you for your courage to pick up your oils first and let your knowledge be your guide in their use.

Preface

This is a book of testimonials about my experiences with oils and animals. I will also share stories from friends that have shared their stories with me. I am an Independent Distributor with Young Living Essential Oils.

The purpose of this information is to give people the confidence to know that they can safely use alternative products for the health and well being of their four-legged friends.

I am not diagnosing or prescribing for your animal's health, your veterinarian will do that for you. This information gives you many options and things to try. Together you and your veterinarian can monitor your progress. You can use many of the oil application ideas with your veterinary treatment, as one can certainly compliment the other in many cases.

Results will vary, animals are different, just as people are. Some are fed healthy diets, some are not. So keep in mind, that the quality of food makes a difference.

It is very important that you use only pure essential oils. Many oils that are offered in health food stores are not 100% pure. There is no standard here in the United States, so legally they need only have 5% essential oil in them and the rest can be synthetic. These oils will not have any healing properties in them. They are good only for aromatherapy. DO NOT INGEST OR PUT ON YOUR SKIN.

Young Living Essential Oils are the only oils I use. Young Living plants, grows, harvests, distills and tests their own oils. They do import some oils, but they are put through rigorous testing. They also have farms in France, China and Ecuador where they grow some of the plants that won't grow in the United States.

The time of day is very important when harvesting the plants to make essential oils. Some must be harvested only in the early morning when the "brick" levels are the highest. Some must be harvested in the evening. The "brick" levels are when the plant's healing qualities are up in the plant and not down in the roots.

I do a lot of work on animals and enjoy sharing with others, to help them gain the knowledge to aid their own animal companions.

It is my experience that many emergencies happen after business hours and on weekends when vets are hard to find, especially in rural areas! These products give us amazing tools to turn a bad situation around.

** The ONLY essential oils I use are the pure essential oils from Young Living Essential Oils. I place most of the oils on neat, without dilution. The hot oils I dilute with either coconut oil or olive oil.

The Main Parts of the Horse

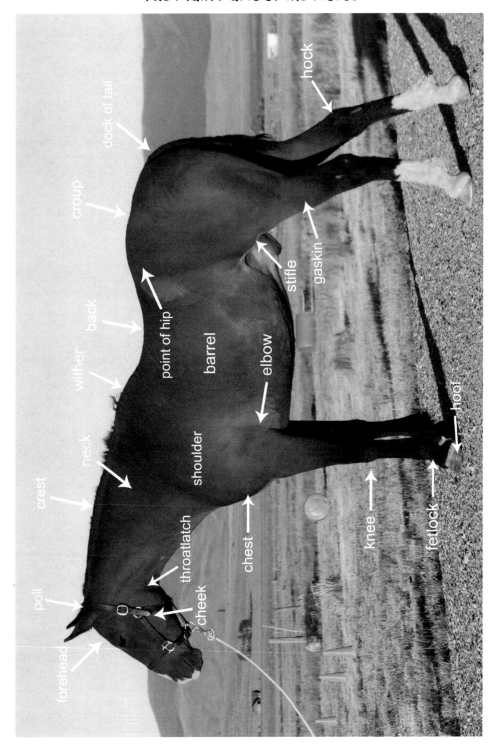

The Main Parts of the Dog

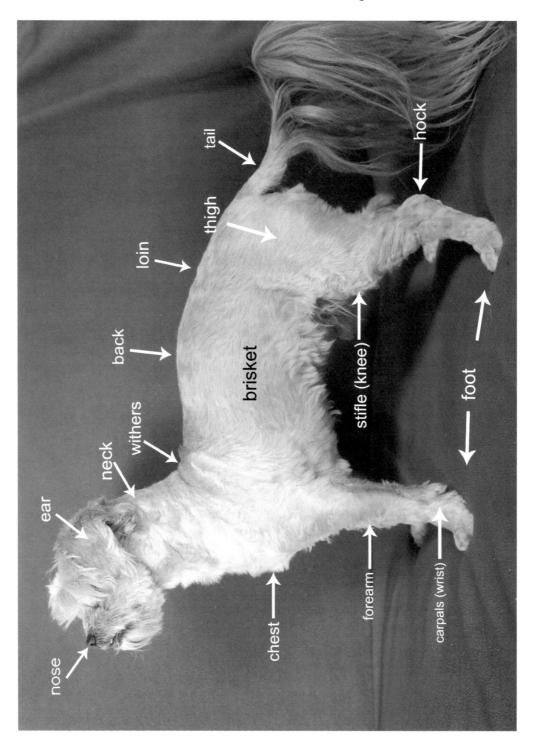

Main Parts of the Cat

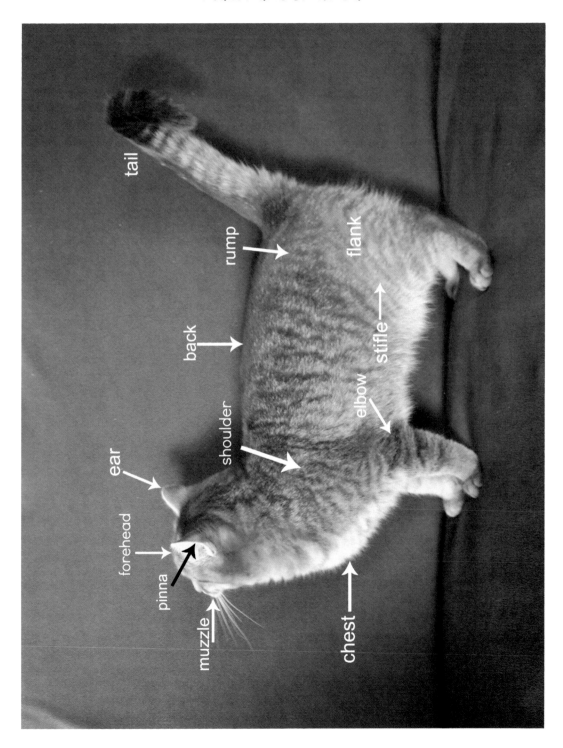

Using a Pendulum

If the thought of using a pendulum makes you uncomfortable just know that you don't have to use one to use the oils. It is simply a tool that can make your use of the oils a bit more accurate. It is definitely NOT a necessity. In fact, if it would make you feel better… feel free to just tear these pages out!

For those of you that do want to use a pendulum, read on!

Thousands of people are familiar and comfortable with the use of Kinesiology/Muscle Testing to test the energy of a person. Many people have seen or experienced the use of the Kirlian Camera that takes pictures of the Aura/Energy Field and the breaks in it that the pictures clearly show. The Pendulum works the same way; it's a tool that can be used to pick up breaks in the energy field of a human or animal, and assist in selecting the oils and supplements that may best aid in repairing the breaks. How does a computer send emails and faxes? How do cell phones get our voices and texts out there on those waves? There aren't even wires! The energy waves are all around us all the time, never ending. The pendulum is a tool to assist in tapping into it. It's not magic, it's science.

To start hold the pendulum in your dominant hand. Hold the pendulum over your non-dominant hand, palm up. Think or say "yes," watch to see if the pendulum starts to swing, and which direction it starts to swing, clockwise or counterclockwise. It is picking up the positive frequency in your body. Mine swings clockwise for "yes."

Next, think or say "no." Watch to see which direction the pendulum swings (or maybe it doesn't swing at all, but just hangs still). Mine swings counterclockwise, picking up the negative frequency.

For some this will start right away, for others it is a little slower. Keep working with it.

To proceed, hold the pendulum as suggested and ask if you are balanced to test. If "yes," proceed. If you get a negative answer then you will have to balance yourself first. This can be done by applying an oil to yourself to raise your frequency. My favorite is *White Angelica*. Other oils like *Peace and Calming*, *Inspiration* or *Highest Potential* are wonderful too.

Now test your balance again.

Ready to proceed?

I only test for health. Ask "yes" and "no" questions only.

Once I have the animal or person either in front of me (in the flesh), in a photograph, or I'm on the phone with them, I am ready to go. I also have a list of oils and supplements in front of me.

To begin, I ask if I have permission to test for this person or animal. If "yes" I go ahead, if "no" I go back to balancing. If I still get a negative, I stop. I ask someone else to test for me. This has happened when I have been sick or too emotionally close to the one in need of testing.

If I don't know where the problem is in the animal, I hold the pendulum over the animal, going from nose to tail, using my non-dominant hand, palm down, between animal and pendulum. If the pendulum is swinging counterclockwise "no," then the issues are not in the spot. It will change and swing "yes," clockwise as soon as you are over an area that needs work.

You can ask which oils would be most beneficial for this animal then go over the oils you have or the oils and supplements on a list. It will swing "yes" over oils and supplements needed and "no" over those not needed.

You can hold the bottle of oil (in your non-dominant hand) over the animal from nose to tail, holding the pendulum over the bottle. It will swing "yes" over the spot where it is needed. Pause there and ask how many drops:

- more than one
- more than two
- more than 3

and on and on until I get a "yes" from the pendulum.

When using supplements, use a list or a bottle and again ask:

- more than one capsule, teaspoon, Tablespoon
- more than two capsules, teaspoons, Tablespoons
- more than three capsules, teaspoons, Tablespoons

This is a short and simple explanation. Experiment, play with it, ask questions in a different way and see if you get the same answer. The frequency is out there, we just have to read it.

I find this way to be most accurate for me. Others are more comfortable with muscle testing. Find what you like. Animals can't talk or point out what is hurting, but this tool has helped me help more animals than I can count!

Section One:

Dogs

"And may we ever have gratitude in our hearts that the great
Creator in all His glory has placed the herbs in the field for our healing."

Dr. Edward Bach

Abscesses:

I have treated with *Melaleuca Alternifolia/TeaTree* to bring it to a head and usually the dog will lick the abscess. This can also be good for them. The taste will discourage them from licking the wound too much.

When the abscess opens I treat it with *Lavender, Melrose* or diluted *Thieves* oil and *Animal Scents Ointment* to speed healing of the tissue.

Agressive Dogs:

In working in my dog kennels I've seen my share of aggressive dogs. I put *Peace and Calming* on me so the dogs can smell it. Then I put *Peace and Calming* in a small mist bottle and mist them directly when they are most aggressive. *Peace and Calming* can also be placed between the pads of their feet and around their ear flap. You may apply this neat. Some dogs don't love *Peace and Calming* so instead you can use *Valor.*

Allergies:

I have noticed that some dogs seem to be allergic to the hairsprays used by their people. Pay attention to where your dog is when you are applying hair products. One dog I was working with had terrible allergies at home. He had terrible itching all over his body. When he came to me for boarding and was outside, his symptoms eased.

The owner was an older woman who sprayed her hair so thoroughly that there was no chance of it moving in a wild breeze. We realized the dog would lay on the floor behind her every morning as she did her hair. The dog laid under the falling hairspray particles and the carpet was loaded with it! His little body was loaded with the toxins from the hairspray. For him I used *Animal Scents Shampoo* and a small amount of *Ningxia Red Juice* to his food.

Some dogs are very sensitive to wheat, beet pulp and corn. If your dog has chronic itchy, dry skin, tearing eyes or chronic ear infections, check the ingredients in your dog food. If you have tried switching food and that has not made a difference, you may have to make your own. This is also great for a dog that is in a weakened condition or for an elderly dog.

Make Your Own Dog Food!

1. Choose one of the following ingredients:
    * Brown Rice
    * Sweet Potato
    * Ground Flax Seed (non GMO)

2. Choose one of the following meats:
    * Fresh Fish (we have used salmon but with the mercury content we now use fresh trout)
    * Venison
    * Chicken
    * Small amounts of Turkey (this can cause gas in dogs)
    * Lamb

3. Then add:
    * Carrots
    * Spinach.

Just throw it all together, add some water and boil or roast it. You can portion it out and freeze it so it lasts longer.

When feeding the individual meal add:
* 1 Tablespoon *Power Meal*
* 1 cap *Sulfurzyme*
* 1 *Super C*
* 1 *Life 5, Vita Green* or *Alfalfa*
* *Ninxia Red Juice* (amount varies with size of dog)
* Blueberries
* Wolfberries

I did this for one little Shih Tzu that I was boarding. He was older, weak and ill, but remained undiagnosed. I started him on this diet and his folks continued it. His health improved dramatically. He lived happily and in good health for 4 more years. In that time he never ate dog food again.

I don't add grains, except for the brown rice, because many dogs are allergic to different grains. Cooking the meat, or using it raw will be up to you.

Anal Glands:

If you notice that your dog has a bloody discharge, that is accompanied by pain when going to the bathroom, check it's anal glands. These are easily expressed. Small dogs should be done once a month. Large dogs don't normally need to be done. If your suspect an infection, you will need to express them once a day.

Then give the dog *Colloidal Silver,* depending on size, 1 to 3 ounces a day. *Lavender* oil mixed with a small amount of V6 applied to the anal area will be soothing.

Arthritis:

I have used *Ortho Sport* which is a wonderful blend for arthritis. I have also put on *Pan Away,* if the pain seems acute.

Idaho Balsam Fir, Wintergreen or *Peppermint* with *Copaiba* layered over the top may also be helpful.

I have added *Power Meal* and *Sulfurzyme* to their food as well.

A *Raindrop Technique* (see page 85) on the hindquarters and hips of many dogs, gently massaging in the oils during the times of acute pain, is also very helpful and soothing.

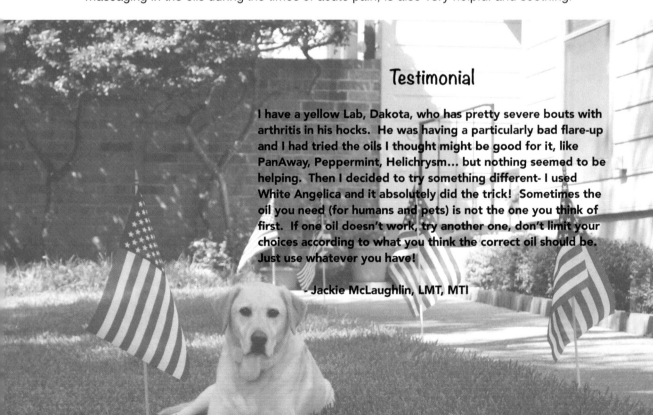

Testimonial

I have a yellow Lab, Dakota, who has pretty severe bouts with arthritis in his hocks. He was having a particularly bad flare-up and I had tried the oils I thought might be good for it, like PanAway, Peppermint, Helichrysm... but nothing seemed to be helping. Then I decided to try something different- I used White Angelica and it absolutely did the trick! Sometimes the oil you need (for humans and pets) is not the one you think of first. If one oil doesn't work, try another one, don't limit your choices according to what you think the correct oil should be. Just use whatever you have!

- Jackie McLaughlin, LMT, MTI

Tick Bites

Tick Bites:

Apply neat directly to the tick bite, any one of these oils, or two at a time:

🐾 Purification
🐾 Thieves
🐾 Mountain Savory
🐾 Oregano
🐾 Thyme

Visit www.aromateam.net for more great tips!

Bee Stings:
One to six drops (depending on size and swelling) of *Purification* directly on the sting followed by the same of *Lavender* applied three times a day or more as needed. I have used this on both people and animals. *Geranium* is also very effective on bee stings, taking the burning sting and itch out of a fresh bee sting.

Ants:
A Golden Retriever had been bitten by a multitude of ants, had a seizure and was presumed dead by her owners. *Purification* and *Lavender* were gently massaged in, all over the muzzle. I applied *Valor*, *Frankincense*, and *Melissa* as well. The dog came out of the stupor and is now healthy and happy.

Bugs:
To help deter bugs from even attaching to your dog you can make a bug spray using:

- 10 drops of *Citronella*
- 10 drops of *Purification*
- 10 drops of *Eucalyptus Citriodora*
- 10 drops of *Peppermint*

Put the drops in a 16 to 24 ounce bottle then fill the rest of the bottle with water and shake well. This works great!

Ticks:
I apply *Purification* or *Thieves* to the tick, to make it back out and then treat the spot with *Purification*. I have also gently pulled the ticks out with tweezers. You can do this if the tick is freshly imbedded. If you aren't sure how long the tick has been in the animal, use the oils for the removal, to avoid leaving parts of the tick in the skin. Another oil you can apply to the entry spot is *Thieves*.

Bleeding:

Geranium, *Helichrysum*, *Wild Tansy*, *Tsuga* or *Cistus* and the powdered Cayenne Pepper all effectively stop bleeding. These work very well on a toe nail clipped too short as well.

Once during grooming, an ear was snipped right along the edge. I tried everything to stop the bleeding, but nothing was working. I heated up a needle and laid it along the edge of the ear, cauterizing it. It worked like a charm. I applied *Lavender* and *Animal Scents Ointment* and the dog never flinched. The owners were pleased and I sent them home with a bottle of *Lavender* and enough ointment for a few days. It healed perfectly, of course.

Cancer: Also see Tumors

I have worked with a couple of dogs who have had cancer. One dog was 18 and had a growth the size of a golf ball on it's hind leg. I was grooming the dog and pointed out several other masses the owner didn't know about. She wanted to keep the dog as comfortable as possible without doing surgery and let the dog go when she felt it was time. We started the oils. The tumor continued to grow slowly over the next two years. We didn't notice an increased growth of the masses on the diaphragm area. The dog continued to eat well, drink and stay hydrated. It stayed active and happy right up until the end.

The owner was applying *Longevity*, *Frankincense*, *Ledum* and *Lavender* on the tumor and other masses. She applied *Peace and Calming* on his feet when he was restless at night. She also gave him six drops of *Longevity* and *Frankincense* in capsules, twice a day. The amount of oil was based on the dog's size, 30 pounds. If she felt the tumor areas were causing problems she would apply *PanAway* to the area. To keep the skin around the large tumor moist and itch free, she applied Olive oil as needed. Last but not least, she added *Ningxia Red Juice* to the dog's food measured at one Tablespoon a day.

Often when cancer is found in dogs it has usually progressed to such a degree that it is difficult to treat. I have seen occasional success. I have also seen dogs pass away, but they have done so with less pain.

Testimonial

A week before Christmas 2008, I took my 16 year old Lab mix, Boo Boo to the vet because of a growth on her foot that had gotten so bad, she couldn't put any weight on it. The growth was due to the fact that she had some long nails and my groomer didn't trim one of them. The nail broke off below the skin. It kept trying to grow back but the new growth always seemed to break off below the skin again.

The vet said the growth was a cancerous tumor and I should put her to sleep right away. She had arthritis and was also blind from cataracts, so he said it would be best to put her to sleep. I said that I had just lost her "brother", my Shepherd/Husky mix to a cancerous tumor in his mouth the previous February and I wasn't going to lose another one before Christmas, so I'd do it after the holidays. I took her home and proceeded to give her the best Christmas I could.

After the holidays, I called some friends and told them of my decision to have Boo Boo put to sleep because of the tumor. They told me about the Young Living Essential Oils and supplements and that even Paul Harvey had talked about how Frankincense oil will kill cancer.

I said that was great, but Boo Boo was 16, blind, arthritic and the tumor was bad enough to where she couldn't put any weight on the foot. They put me in touch with their uplink who is a nurse and a healer. She had me take pictures of Boo Boo's foot and email them, along with the pictures I had taken of her on Christmas Eve. She said that we would start treating the tumor and the arthritis and once the cancer was gone, we would treat the cataracts. So I ordered Ningxia Red, Sulfurzyme, BLM supplements and Frankincense and Balsam Fir oils. Then started the treatments on January 12th. I mixed the Ningxia Red, Sulfurzyme and BLM in her canned food twice a day. I put 10 drops of each of the oils on the tumor three times a day.

The change in my old dog was amazing. She had more energy and started hopping around the yard on three legs. By January 23rd, the tumor was half it's original size. I continued with the treatments and she seemed to be improving. The tumor kept getting smaller. By February 12th, the tumor was less than a quarter of it's original size.

Sadly, unknown to anyone, the cancer had moved from Boo Boo's foot into the rest of her body. She started going downhill and crossed the Rainbow Bridge on February 12th. Although she died, this is a success story. Working through the Young Living products, God gave me almost two more months with my precious dog than the vet said we'd have. She died at home, on her bed, in my arms instead of on the floor in some vet's office.

- Kim, Merritt Island, FL

Top Photo: The tumor when the dog was first taken to the vet.

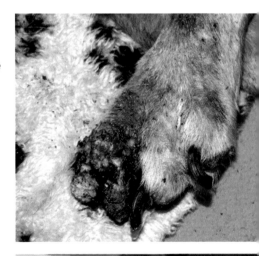

Middle Photo: A month later

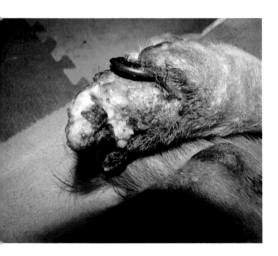

Bottom Photo: Taken just a bit before she was put down.

Cold and Flu:

As well as the recommendations in the EODR (Essential Oil Desk Reference), I add *Super C* to their food and Silver Water or Colloidal Silver to their water dish. Now that Young Living has come out with *Thieves Household Cleaner* I would add that to their water dish. *Eucalyptus*, *Melalueca* or the oil blends of *R.C.* or *Raven* may be rubbed onto the chest area and *Thieves* on their feet. *Exodus II* diluted with Olive oil or V6 mixing oil applied around the ears. *Longevity* (dilute this one too, it has *Thyme* in it, which can get hot) on the spine. Diffusing *R.C.* or *Raven* in the room where the dog stays also works well.

I have also used the oils internally with dogs by choosing either *Longevity* or *Thieves* and putting from three to ten drops in a capsule, depending on the weight of the dog. Three drops for the little guys and up to ten drops for the larger breeds. You can then pop the capsule down their gullet, either by hiding the capsule in a little butter, or a piece of meat, or a soft treat. If you don't have all of these oils, that's OK, just use what you have! Depending on the degree of the cold or flu you can use just one or two oils.

Depression:

I have noticed that some dogs just seem to fall into a depression. It can be from boredom, lack of exercise, being left behind at a boarding kennel, the loss of a buddy, or the loss of an owner. I have used the oil blend *Hope* on some, applying it to their feet and heart. *Joy* is another one that works well.

Diarrhea:

Di-Gize or *Peppermint* may be rubbed on the stomach. For a dog that has chronic diarrhea and seems to be too thin, *Detoxzyme* may be of great assistance as well as *Life 5*. With many dogs their bodies are not producing enough digestive enzymes and their food is running right through them. I have noticed this to be especially common with Dobermans. *Essentialzyme* is a must here, as it contains the Pancreatic enzymes they require. Canned pumpkin mixed in their food can also help firm up the stool.

Disinfecting Dog Toys:

Disinfecting Puppy Toys:

You can either drop a few drops of Thieves into a small bucket of warm water and allow the toys to soak for 10 minutes, then wipe dry. Or you can simply spray them with Thieves Household Cleaner and wipe dry with a clean rag!

a few drops of this

please visit www.aromateam.net for more great tips!

or spray this!

Ears:

Many dogs suffer from ear infections. Try a couple of drops of *Lavender* and *Melaleuca* in a teaspoon of Olive oil or V6 oil and drip this just inside the ear, around the lower portion. Then massage the ear together and up against the head. Also put Helichrysum down the outside of the ear along the Eustachian Tube area and massage it in. If the ear is badly infected any touch may be difficult.

To make a spray use your little bottle of *Thieves spray* with just about a half inch of the spray in the bottom of the bottle add:

- One Tablespoon of Olive oil
- Three drops of *Lemon Grass*
- Four drops of *Copaiba*
- Five drops of *Purification*

Then fill the remainder with distilled water, shake well and spray into the ear. Be sure to shake well before each application.

Another treatment is two drops of *Frankincense* oil mixed with one teaspoon of V6 oil, dropped down the inside of the back edge of the ear. I have also added Silver Water in the ear and also in the dog's water dish with very good results.

Melrose is great for ear mites. *Peppermint* or *Purification* diluted with Olive oil on a q-tip swabbed into the ear is also very effective. Don't go too deep, just swab the part of the ear you can see.

To clean the ears apply coconut oil to the inside of the ear flap. Coconut oil is very soothing to the ears. It's also an anti fungal and anti bacterial and will last for two years on the counter before going rancid. It melts at 75 degrees, so will become liquid in your hands.

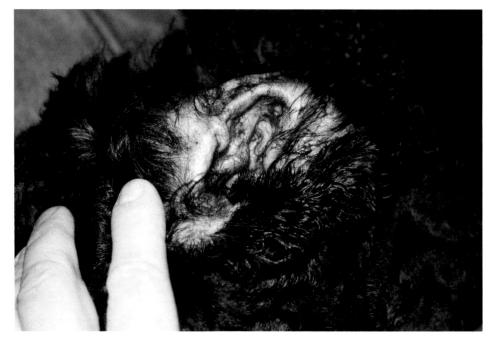

An infected ear.

Two weeks after treatment with coconut oil and the *Thieves* Spray mix.

Eyes, Tearing:

Sulfurzyme works great when you add it to your dog's food. For small dogs you would add just a quarter of a teaspoon, lessen that amount if you notice loose stools.

Also *Di-Gize* may be beneficial. This would go on the dogs feet in between the pads once every other day for the first week, then once a week.

Some dog food ingredients such as beet pulp, grains, or yeast can cause tearing, so check your dog food bag!

Falls and Body Trauma:

I have a dog that fell off the stairs to the ground five feet below, when she was a small puppy. She did a twist in the air and landed on her head, neck and left hip. I applied *M-Grain* to her head and *PanAway* to her neck and hip. She wouldn't put weight on her hind leg, so I also layered *Aroma Siez*, *Wintergreen* and *Peppermint*. I thought she may have thrown her back out a bit so I put *Valor* into the pad area of her feet, on her shoulders and on both hips. I did this three times the first day and twice the second. By that evening she didn't even limp. We never saw any swelling. *Trauma Life* would have been very helpful to put on my hands and cup over her nose while she was still shrieking in fear and pain. I highly recommend it and now have it on hand at all times.

Fear:

I have worked with several dogs that were high strung and fearful. Some were afraid of loud noises and some had a fear of horses. To combat their fear I have used *Valor* on their spine and feet and a drop of *White Angelica* on each shoulder.

Peace and Calming on the inner earflap and on the feet is also very relaxing. *Chivalry* and/or *Highest Potential* applied to the top of the head and down the neck will also support the dog during stressful times. A drop of *Believe* on the webbing of each paw can be very relaxing.

Peppermint on the paws and Colloidal Silver are both helpful for fighting off viruses or bacteria. You can freeze the Colloidal Silver in ice cube trays to make feeding easier. Some dogs really love crunching the ice cubes. Another wonderful supplement to add to their food is *Ninxgia Red Juice* or the *Wolfberries*.

Fever:

Peppermint on the paws and Colloidal Silver are both helpful for fighting off viruses or bacteria. You can freeze the Colloidal Silver in ice cube trays to make feeding easier. Some dogs really love crunching the ice cubes. Another wonderful supplement to add to their food is *Ninxgia Red Juice* or the *Wolfberries*.

Food Choices and Management:

Raw diets are great but for some people it is too much to do on their own and can be expensive to feed. We do what we can for our beloved pets. We research and learn what to avoid and what to look for.

When I was running a kennel I used high quality dry foods, offering raw treats now and then. A trick to feeding raw treats is to feed them BEFORE you feed the dry food. Dry dog food can take as long as 15 hours to digest while raw food only takes about 4-6 hours. Therefore if you feed dry food before the raw treat, the raw will sit behind the dry food causing upset tummies, diarrhea and discomfort. This is because the raw food is slowly turning rancid while waiting to be digested.

Soy is an undigestible protein and is an ingredient in many dog foods, so be sure to read the ingredient list! It just moves through the dog's system without providing any nutritional value. Some dogs are also allergic to soy. It's best to steer clear of it all together.

Our dogs rely on us to provide a healthy and nutritional food option. So it's up to us to do the research and read the labels! For instance, the moist chewy food that looks so appealing is actually soft because of harmful chemicals such as Propylene Glycol, which is a fancy term for Antifreeze.

Portion sizes are very important for the health of our dogs as well. Many people are slowly killing their dogs with kindness. Feeding leftovers from our table does not actually make for a healthy dog. It can lead to obesity and digestive problems. Your dog may beg for more food just after he finishes his serving, but he does not need it. An overweight dog is at risk for all kinds of health problems such as Diabetes, hip and knee problems, back problems and a shortened life span.

To put it simply, less is more! Research, research, research!

Grieving:

If you have not seen an animal grieve, consider yourself lucky! Dogs grieve the loss of a loved one just as we do. Symptoms of grief are depression, refusing to eat, whining and sleeping more.

To help them through this you can apply *Peace and Calming* to the pads of their feet, put some in your hand and stroke through your dog's hair coat. This will not only support them through this time, but will help family members as well in the form of aromatherapy to those in the room.

Joy on their heart area is also helpful. I did this for a poodle mix whose human mother passed away. She was immediately brought to my house for boarding while the family gathered. This little dog knew what happened and she was grieving seriously. Not only did she lose her mom, she was removed from the comfort of her home and her extended human family. I oiled her often, then sent her home well oiled. Her dad told me later she smelled wonderful and he liked holding her close because she made him feel better. Since then I have had three other dogs arrive during a time of grief and have done the same with them.

Hearing:

I worked on a six month old puppy that had been deaf since birth. I put one drop of *Helichrysum* along the inner edge of each ear and massaged it in thoroughly. She shook her head a lot for the first couple of minutes. I suspect it may have been a bit uncomfortable.

The second day as I examined her ears, there was a plug of yuck in one. When I removed it, a large amount of green slime started coming out of her ear. I swabbed the goo out and was amazed by the amount that continued to come out. When it was finally clear I checked the other ear and it was clean. I applied another drop of *Helichrysum* to each ear and massaged again. She went home after that treatment and returned two days later for another one. The other ear had a small amount of dried matter in it, which I cleaned out, then reapplied the oil. Her owners were thrilled! The dog could now hear! The sound of her own bark scared her so much, she stopped barking for three weeks!

She had an infection deep within her Eustachian tube. This caused her to appear deaf and probably also caused quite a lot of pain. She would never let anyone scratch her under her chin and she hated wearing a collar, collapsing whenever a leash was attached. This all changed dramatically after her oiling. Though she didn't know what any sounds or words meant, she caught on quickly. I treated her once a week for two more weeks and she continued to improve, until she was 100%.

Heart Problems:

For dogs with heart issues you can apply *Cardio Care* to the dog once at 3am and again eleven hours later at 2pm. For small to medium dogs you could do the application every 10 hours. Applying *Aroma Life* to their heart area would also be beneficial.

In the past I have started a few of my boarding dogs on this regiment at the their owners request. We found the coughing from the congestive heart failure to ease. Once they were more stable we were able to lessen the application to once a day.

For more severe cases, stick to twice a day.

Hip-Dysplasia:

To ease the discomfort of hip-dysplasia I have layered *Aroma Siez*, *PanAway* and *Copaiba* mixed with V6 on the groin, *Ortho Sport* on the hips and added the supplements *Sulfurzyme*, *Super C* and *Vita Greens* to their diet.

For less severe cases you can add the supplement *Sulfurzyme* to their diet with good results.

Hyper Bouncy:

For the dog that is driving you nuts with it's inability to calm down, try applying *Peace and Calming* to the feet and chest. If you have a dog that is reactive to *Peace and Calming*, then use *Valor* on the feet and chest instead.

Gentle Baby has also proven to be beneficial. You can offer this in your hands for the dog to lick if it would. You can also apply it to the dog's gums. You can use *Roman Chamomile* in place of *Gentle Baby* as well.

Puppyhood is a great time to get your dog used to having it's feet handled. Putting oils on their feet is a wonderful way to introduce having their feet touched. This can translate into your dog being more agreeable to having it's feet groomed/clipped and having it's toe nails trimmed.

Impaction/Constipation:

I took care of two five-week old Pomeranian puppies, one weighed approximately one pound and the other even less. The owner had started them on an inexpensive solid adult dog food. This very inexpensive adult dog food was loaded with soy which is used as a cheap filler by some dog food companies. As we discussed before soy is not digestible by dogs.

Both of the puppies became severely impacted. The larger female was not in quite as dire straits as the little one, but neither one could have a bowel movement. They were both very sore, with distended back ends. The tiny one was in severe pain, with glazed eyes and an inability to walk. I didn't think she would survive.

I started them both on a regiment. First I applied an enema, using a 3 ml syringe, a neutralizer along with two drops of a gentle soap and a bit of moisturizing gel. Another option would be to use warm water with coconut oil and *Mineral Essence* for the enema. Then I applied a drop of *DiGize* on each puppy's belly twice a day.

The bigger puppy started having bowel movements within fifteen minutes. The smaller puppy didn't improve as quickly. When I would give her the enemas the liquid would leak back out, but I had faith that my efforts would pay off so I stayed diligent.

I continued this treatment three to four times a day and on the second day, the smaller puppy started getting rid of a bit of the build up, but she had no control, it would just leak out of her. At least it was beginning to come out!

I started feeding them both Gerber's baby rice cereal, Gerber's baby chicken, yogurt, two drops of *Mineral Essence*, a sprinkle of *Super Cal* and a dash of *Power Meal*.

The bigger puppy bounced back quickly and was going to the bathroom on her own by the third day. By the fourth day we started to see a positive change in the smaller puppy as well. We stopped giving her the enemas, her appetite increased, her eyes brightened, but she still couldn't walk.

It took about eight days for her to really turn around, but she did! She started out standing, then walking for short periods before she needed to sit and rest. Her vision was perfect. She was playful and adorable.

The smaller puppy was the youngest, tiniest puppy I have worked with.

Injury:

For immediate response to an injury I put *Trauma Life* on my hands, then cup them over the nose of the dog. I also put *Gentle Baby* on the ears, assess the injuries and call the vet.

Insecurity:

Many animals experience this. Some have developed it at the hand of a cruel uncaring master, some have been rescued from shelters and they don't trust humans. For these dogs I will begin by diffusing *Peace and Calming* in the room. I will also drop some oils in their bedding, *Peace and Calming*, *Believe* or *Transformation*.

I have also used *Trauma Life*, *Release*, *Hope* and *Joy* on the feet and heart areas.

I also have the oils on my hands whenever I go to handle or work with them.

You can apply these oils over the first few weeks as the animal adjusts.

Kennel Cough:

Kennel cough is a contagious respiratory ailment frequently picked up at veterinary clinics and boarding kennels. Though I never had an outbreak at my kennel, my parents had a dog that contracted this after being at an out-of-state boarding kennel. We began the regiment by diffusing *Thieves* and *RC* mixed together in the diffuser, in a small room where we were keeping the dog.

We then layered *Lavender, Lemon, Lemongrass, Mountain Savory, Peppermint,* and *Oregano* along the spine, dropping the oils then massaging them into the skin. I diluted the mixture with some olive oil because of the heat caused by *Lemongrass* and *Oregano.* I then applied *Rosemary* and *Myrtle* to his paws, massaging it in between his pads. His coughing began to subside.

We did this for two days after which we simply applied *RC* and *Raven* to his chest twice a day for the next four days. We also added a couple drops of *Thieves Household Cleaner* to his drinking water and *Mineral Essence* to his food. In a week he was bouncing around, bright eyed and bushy tailed!

Kidneys/Bladder:

I have used *K & B* for dogs with kidney or bladder problems. I would also massage two to five drops of the *Inspiration Blend* or layer *Juniper, Ledum* or *Geranium* over the kidney areas.

I applied one drop of each oil for the small animals and two to five drops for the larger ones, once a day, and the results have been excellent!

Nervous Anxiety:

Some signs of nervous anxiety are heavy panting, drooling, licking, chewing their feet, biting, pacing, whining and extreme shedding. I worked with one extremely nervous dog who was to be in some summer dog shows to finish getting her points, after having a few years off.

I started her on a regiment of applying *White Angelica* on her shoulders, *Peace and Calming* on her paws, *Believe* on her head, *Joy* on her heart and *Valor* down her spine daily for a couple weeks before her show.

During this time her owner began taking her on practice car rides as well as journeys to public parks to prepare for the business of the show grounds. She noted that the dog's attitude was much calmer during these practice car rides and sessions with the aid of the oils. When the shows began, the dog breezed through the season and finished a champion.

Odor Control:

When your dog is difficult to sit next to because of the smells emanating from him, check the mouth for sores and/or bad teeth. For this issue it's best to have a veterinarian take a look. Infection of the teeth or gums can lead to heart issues, so can be a very serious problem. As a follow up regiment you can occasionally brush the dogs teeth with the *Dentarome* toothpaste. Once a week brushings can be beneficial. Dogs have good bacteria in their mouths that is necessary for keeping their teeth and gums healthy. We don't want to brush that away!

Another wonderful remedy for sore gums is *Thieves Fresh Essence Mouthwash*. I would dip a q-tip in the mouthwash and apply it to the gums daily, until the soreness dissipates.

I have checked a dog's mouth and found a stick wedged up between the back teeth and into the roof of the mouth. This caused wounds on the tongue and roof of the mouth that were infected and sore. We applied *Thieves* to the inside of the dog's mouth using *Thieves* mixed with a small amount of water, shaken and sprayed into the dog's mouth. The dog didn't love our remedy, but it worked! The dog's mouth healed and he went on to chew up more sticks.

Another reason dogs can be smelly is that they have a problem digesting their food properly. I have added the supplement *Detoxyme* to their food to aid in digesting. *Detoxyme* helps the dog's body utilize the food better, which in turn will reduce odor.

Parasites:

Parasites are a serious problem for dogs. Dogs love to scavenge. Always looking for things to put in their mouth, horse manure, sheep manure, deer manure, etc, etc. It is easy for them to pick up parasites this way!

I have used *ParaFree* capsules, given orally with great results. *DiGize* rubbed on the dog's tummy also works well. The amount used varies with the size of the dog.

For a 7 to 10 pound dog I have poked a hole in a capsule and squeezed out 2 drops of *ParaFree* and administered it twice a day for five days, given them a couple days break, then given it again for five days.

A 10 to 20 pound dog again, I would poke a hole in the capsule and administer 5 drops two times daily for five days, give them a couple of days rest, then administer again for five days.

For a 20 to 50 pound dog administer eight drops, twice a day for five days, give them a couple days off, then administer for five more days.

A dog over 50 pounds I would give one capsule twice a day for five days, then a couple days break, then again for five days.

Parvovirus:

Parvovirus can be a quick killer therefore it can take a lot of work to save your puppy or dog if they contract this virus. Parvo is highly contagious, easily picked up and carried home on the bottom of your shoes, after a vet visit, or after visiting a litter of puppies that may have the virus and even your local shelter. It's a good idea to have *Thieves Household Cleaner* in your car so you can spray the bottom of the shoes after you leave the vet clinic, before you get back in your car. If you visit a shelter or a breeder's place you should spray your shoes again, **before** getting into your car. This will ensure that you don't bring the virus home!

If you do end up with a puppy or dog that contracts this virus, veterinary care is crucial. If you recognize the symptoms and are not able to get to a veterinarian right away, know that there is hope. Here is what I did.

I started with five drops of *DiGize* on the puppy's stomach and feet. I applied this every four hours. Then I mixed *Thieves* and olive oil in a syringe and administered this by mouth once every hour for four hours and then once every two hours until it was not needed.

Next I applied *Exodus II* on the puppy's feet three times during the day, while also diffusing *Exodus II*, until I ran out, then I diffused *Thieves* being sure that the diffuser was running at all times.

I applied *Thieves* and *Exodus II* on the spine, dropping a few drops on the spine, then massaging them in. I then added a bit of olive oil to soothe the skin, because these are hot oils.

I also forced Silver Water by mouth, using a syringe, every half hour for the first two hours. Now I would use water mixed with *Mineral Essence*, *Life 5* and *Ningxia Red Juice*. Hydration is crucial at this stage. It's amazing how quickly a dog can become dehydrated, weaken and slip away. Then I backed off and forced liquid every hour attempting to get the puppy to swallow one to two ounces on his own, each time. I did this four times a day for the first day.

As the puppy began to improve, instead of feeding it puppy food, we mixed up baby rice cereal, with yogurt and one teaspoon of *Power Meal* to gently introduce it's stomach to solid food.

When this puppy came in for boarding and I realized that it did indeed have Parvo, I immediately began the above regiment. I had another dog boarding at the kennel at the time that also had to be inside, so to ensure that she didn't also get Parvo, I began diffusing *Thieves* into her crate while also misting her with a *Thieves*/water spray. I also put *DiGize* on her tummy a couple of times in the night.

The next morning, as soon as I was able, I got the puppy to a veterinarian who took over his care. It turned out that all he needed was some I.V. fluids, after all I had administered throughout the night. The vet was impressed!

Passing Away:

When I have had to assist my dogs over the Rainbow Bridge I have found that applying *Peace and Calming* to the head and paws, *Joy* on the heart, *Believe* to the back of the neck and *Transformation* to the top of the head before making the trip to the vet, or having the vet out, helps both of us feel better about the trip ahead. This has helped my dogs feel less anxious about being at the vet as well.

Porcupine Quills:

I've pulled many quills out of many dogs. I've found that some dogs learn the first time. Other dogs get angry and seek revenge. These are the repeat offenders.

Seeking veterinary care is ideal. However, if your dog doesn't have too many quills, or it's the middle of the night, just know that I have been known to remove them myself.

I have a pair of pliers handy. Some people will cut off the end of the quill, feeling that it releases pressure and helps in the removal. I don't usually do that as keeping the end on gives me more to hang onto while I'm pulling them out.

First I will apply *Peace and Calming* to the pad of the dog's feet, four drops each, then also to the ear flaps. I'll put *Trauma Life* in my hands and hold it in front of the dog as well, you can also drop about four drops right on the muzzle if the quills are taking up all the room on the dogs nose.

I would seek help at this point, preferably a strong man, to hold the dog down while I started pulling the quills out.

When the quills had gone into the dog's mouth I would remove them by pulling from the interior end of the quill, the end that is brown and sharp.

After the quills have been removed I would bathe the area with *Thieves Household Cleaner, Thieves* or *Lavender Foaming Hand Wash.* I would then apply *Purification* or *Melrose* and *Animal Scents Ointment.*

Pregnancy:

When I had a pregnant dog I liked to add a nice hearty stew to her menu about a week prior to her delivery date. I would supplement her with *Mineral Essence*, *Super Cal* and *Power Meal*. You can adjust the amounts according to your dog's weight.

When a dog is within 24 hours of giving birth, her body temperature will usually drop to about 93 degrees.

After she had the puppies I continued to supplement her for as long as she was nursing. I would offer her a treat, two Tablespoons of yogurt or cottage cheese periodically throughout the time that she was nursing as well.

When I noticed that my dog was suffering from mastitis I had to relieve the pressure by expressing the milk by hand until it was empty. Afterward I would massage the area with *Lavender* oil. This must be done several times a day until the teat fills with clean milk. From experience, if you happen to express it onto a wooden deck, it will seal the wood for a good three years!

Seizures/ Stroke:

I worked on one dog five days after her stroke. First, I applied *Peace and Calming* on her tongue and chest and I let that set for a minute before I moved onto anything else. Second, I applied four drops each of, *Valor* to her feet, *M-Grain* on the top of her head and *Clarity* from the base of her neck up to the base of her skull. Lastly I put one drop of *Brain Power* on her tongue.

She had lost most of the use of her hind legs immediately after the stroke. After the oil application she regained use of her hind legs. They were very weak, so I layered *Oregano*, *Thyme*, *Wintergreen* and *Basil* from her tail to mid spine, then applied *Ortho Ease* to her hips.

When I checked back the next day, she was 100% and back to normal.

I have used the same oils for seizures as for strokes.

When I worked on another dog, within fifteen minutes of two Grand Mal Seizures I put *Peace and Calming* on his chest, then opened his mouth and put a drop of *Brain Power* on his tongue. I then put *Valor* on his feet and several drops of *Frankincense* on his head.

The owners saw a remarkable change in him on the return drive home. He had been laying on the seat and suddenly jumped up to look out the window, barking at the dogs he saw on his way home. He has continued in good health since.

If I had a dog with these same symptoms I would now introduce, *Ningxia Red Juice* or *Wolfberries*, *Sulfurzyme*, and *OmegaGize* as supplements to the dog's diet. Amounts would vary by the dog's weight. *OmegaGize* contains Omega 3's and CO-Q10 which provide support to the brain health.

Tendons and Ligaments:

When I had a dog strain it's knee (stifle area) I mixed equal amounts of *Lemongrass* and *Lavender* and applied it right to the injured area. Keep in mind, if the dog shows discomfort after the application of *Lemongrass* or *PanAway* they can be a little hot, so dilute with olive oil.

I have also used *Spruce*, *White Fir*, *PanAway*, *Copaiba* and *Pine* layered on the sprained area. Remember any oil is better than no oil, so try what you have on hand!

Testimonial

Hi Sara,
I am currently reading your book "Natural Health Care For Your Four Legged Friends"(first edition) and I was wondering if you could advise an oil or blend for my situation. My large dog had TPLO surgery two weeks ago and has quite a seroma. I'm using massage and trying cold and heat packs, but he is resisitant. Will any oils help dissipate the fluid? I use only Young Living as well. I thought maybe Tangerine and Frankincense? I'd love your opinion. Thank you. Also, how often to apply?
Thanks again.
Lisa

Hi Lisa,
If it were me...I would try Palo Santo. I would start with 13 drops. Gently massage that in, then apply a cold pack for about 5 minutes, then a hot pack for about 15 and repeat cold and heat three more times. You can do this twice a day if you wish. I'm not prescribing, just suggesting. Personally, with the issues that caused the problem and to assist healing, movement and comfort level down the road, people have found an 1/8 tsp of YL's BLM and 3 Sulfurzyme caps supplemented to the dog's food, to be very helpful.
Sara

Hi Sara,
Thank you very much. I started him on BLM this week and I may add Sulfurzyme as well. I appreciate your input! I'll keep you posted!
Lisa

Hi Sara,
Just thought I would let you know that a few months ago I messaged you about what YL oil to use on my dog who had TPLO surgery and had a large seroma. You recommended Palo Santo to bring down that swelling. I wanted to let you know that it worked and he is fully recovered and we are so happy to have our boy back!! Thank you for your recommendation and taking the time to hep us out. It is much appreciated!
Lisa

Hi Lisa,
Thank you for sharing that with me!! I'm so glad to hear that it was successful!!!! I love to hear outcomes!!!!!
Sara

Thyroid:

I have groomed many dogs that had thyroid disorders as it's very common in dogs. I would see it more in those that weren't eating very high quality food. A dog with thyroid trouble often presents with these symptoms:

- overweight (particularly the front end)
- their hair usually starts thinning (they may get bald patches)
- the skin can become red, irritated and scaly with small sores
- sometimes the dog can be very underweight
- some may have itchy feet with bald spots

Thyromin is my go-to for dogs with these symptoms. I worked together with a dog owner and we started his dog on *Thryomin* and *Ningxia Red Juice*. He saw a marked improvement in his dog's skin and hair coat.

Tumors: Also see Cancer

I worked on a dog that had tumors in the mammary area. I layered *Frankincense* and *Purification* on the tumors. The tumors became noticeably smaller.

I also worked on a dog that had cancer in the cartilage of her nose. The owner used *Frankincense*, dropping it on her nose from tip to head, then rubbing it in. Then she would drop *Patchouly* on in the same fashion. She would apply *Helichrysum* as needed, to help control the dog's pain. It slowed the growth down and helped her breathe more freely.

Vaccinations:

I no longer have any of my animals vaccinated. When I explain my reason to the veterinarians they never argue or dispute my decision. However, many people live in town and have to for licensing. Some people travel with their dogs and need to vaccinate. Others have show dogs and must vaccinate them as well. You can support your dogs during this time by supplementing their diet with *Ningxia Red Juice*, adding it to their food for a week before vaccinations and a week after.

I also like to give a *Raindrop Technique* (see page 85) before vaccinating. This supports their immune system during this time.

Testimonial

I have a Shih Tzu-Poodle that is six pounds fully grown. When little Stella was getting her shots as a baby, I brought her in for her second round of shots. The nurse and Dr. failed to read her chart at all and re-vaccinated her for rabies. Thank goodness this did not kill her, because it could have. Two days after the shot, hair fell out. Her whole hind quarters were naked and exposed raw skin. We were first very scared, second very angry, third very smart for being a Young Living user and lover. I took my handy dandy pet ointment mixed in a drop of melrose and applied every day. Within two days you could tell in the skin that it was healing and within two months all of her hair was back. You can not tell where it was at all, again, thank goodness. Stella loves her oils, every time I give a massage or get them out she wants to be around them.

Lemongrass works great for fleas.

Animal Scents ointment also works wonders for when your little furry one has a belly ache or is just not feeling all that great. Within half an hour they will back to normal, playing and running around.

Young Living is #1 in our house for everything we need.

Thanks,

Alexis Monroe

Vomiting:

When I have had dogs that could not stop vomiting first I had my veterinarian check it over. There could be many reason for this, one of them is ingesting a bacteria through the many things they put in their mouth and snarf down before we can get to them!

To help my dog I first began fasting him, as per my veterinarian's recommendation. Fasting can be tricky so it's best to do this under the direction of your vet.

To help my dog be more comfortable I applied *DiGize* on his tummy several times a day until the vomiting stopped.

I applied *Peace and Calming* to his paws, massaging it in between his pads. I layered *Lemon* over the *Peace and Calming* as well.

Wounds, Cuts, Abrasions:

When our dog was shot with a pellet gun by a neighbor, of course she ended up with a big sore. The first thing I did was bathe the area with 10 drops of *Lavender,* a Tablespoon of *Animal Scents Shampoo* and mixed that with water. I gently washed the area to remove all the dirt and debris.

Then I layered the following oils:

- *Melrose*
- *Wild Tansy*
- *Helichrysum* (this will stop bleeding and reduce pain)
- *White Fir*
- *Melaleuca*

Lastly, I covered the wound with *Animal Scents Ointment* to seal and protect the wound.

Essential Oils and Acupressure for Dogs

Dogs who have pain or are recovering from injury can benefit from a combination of Young Living's essential oils and acupressure. Practitioners of canine acupressure believe the flow of blood to the injured area can heal muscles or ligaments, joints, scarring and some chronic conditions. We know essential oil applications work and are enhanced by acupressure.

Acupressure helps to improve the quality of life in elderly dogs suffering from hip dysplasia, arthritis, as well as every day aches and pains. At the same time, it can calm a new puppy and help ease the transition period.

We will be doing acupressure with Young Living's Essential Oils. This is what I use:

- Strengthening the immune system, reducing inflammation: *ImmuPower, Thieves*
- Strengthening, muscles, tendons, joints and bones: *Valor, PanAway, Deep Relief, Copaiba*
- Releasing natural cortisone (which alleviates inflammation and swelling): *Copaiba, Pine*
- Releasing endorphins (instrumental in calming and relieving pain): *PanAway, Helichrysm*
- Sharpening mental focus: *Clarity, Brain Power*
- Increasing circulation: *Aroma Life, Cypress*
- Removing toxins: *Helichrysm, Juva Cleanse, Juva Flex*
- Alleviating anxiety: *Acceptance, Believe, Forgiveness, Hope, Peace and Calming, Valor*
- Helping with behavioral issues: *Believe, Clarity, Dragon Time, Peace and Calming, Valor*
- Improving digestion: *DiGize, Peppermint*

Acupressure is not a difficult process. It can be applied in the position that your dog likes best: standing, sitting or laying down.

1. Help your dog get ready for the experience by petting and massaging his favorite spots.

2. Now determine which pressure area and essential oil could bring comfort to your dog:
    - our graphic shows some general points
    - if you do muscle testing, find the point, then test for it
    - your pet can help you find the point, especially if it's sensitive or hurting

3. Once you have located the point, apply one to three drops of your chosen essential oil and then apply steady, gentle pressure with your thumb or index finger. As you do this visualize an even flow of energy going through that point, into your dog's body.

4. Increase the pressure and release it after five to fifteen seconds, don't hold for any longer. If your dog feels uncomfortable, release the pressure. If you come across the tender spot, simply massage the tender area and as the dog relaxes, slowly apply pressure to that point. Acupressure can also be done on cats, horses and other pets.

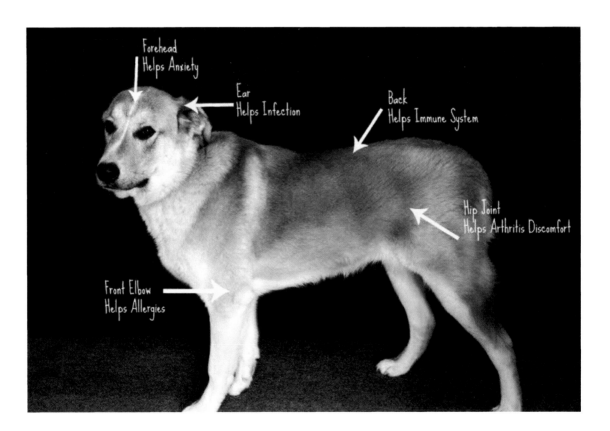

Section Two

Cats

"To keep the body in good health is a duty...
otherwise we shall not be able to keep our mind strong and clear."

– Buddha

There is a lot of negative press out there about using essential oils on cats. Some of it may be true, in cases where people are using oils other than Young Living Essential Oils.

I have used the Young Living Essential Oils on cats for years and had great results. We have had two cats live long into old age, one into her 20's and the other is 18 years old. We had them both from kitten hood, so they were raised in a house where we diffused and applied oils daily, with no adverse reactions!

I now have three cats and at least one can be found in my oil application room, in my home, whenever someone comes in for a *Raindrop Technique* (see page 85). My cats love the oils. They come in and sleep on the massage table in-between clients.

Abscesses:

When I've had cats come in from their outdoor adventures with abscesses I have a few go-to oils that I've had wonderful success with.

First I applied *Purification* and *Thieves* to the abscess to help bring it to a head. Once the abscess opened then I washed the area with *Thieves Household Cleaner*.

Follow up procedure has been to layer on *Lavender* and *Purification*. I then put a thin layer of *Animal Scents Ointment* over the wound to seal it and help keep it clean.

Aggressive Cats:

When I have boarded some cats with attitude problems, with the owner's permission, I have applied 2 drops of *Peace and Calming* to the cat's paws. One specific cat was really becoming aggressive toward it's people, so I had the owners apply 2 drops of *Peace and Calming* to each paw for two weeks. After that regiment the cat calmed down and became peaceful again.

Allergies/ Cat Food:

I have noticed that some cats seem to be very sensitive to the chemicals that their humans use, hairspray, perfume, lotions, etc. If you notice that your cat has hair loss, excessive itching, or hot spots try removing them from the room when you apply your hairspray and maybe back off the perfume… oils work wonderfully as an all natural perfume!

Some cats are very sensitive to wheat, beet pulp, and yeast that can be found in their food. It's important to read the labels on the food that you are offering your cat.

If you have tried switching food and are still having problems, you can make your own!
To begin with, blend these ingredients together in a blender (after cooking):

Choose one of the the following:
- Brown Rice
- Sweet Potato
- Ground Flax Seed (choose non GMO)

Choose one of the following meats:
- Fresh fish (we have used salmon but due to the mercury we now use Fresh Trout)
- Venison
- Chicken
- Turkey
- Lamb

Then add:
- Carrots
- Spinach

You can portion it out and freeze the meals individually. When you feed it to your cat, you can add *Ningxia Red Juice* or *Wolfberries* to the food.

Arthritis:

As our cats have aged they have slowed down. If they seem more sore than normal, and I suspect arthritis, I will apply *Copaiba*, dripping on the affected area and then massaging it in.

I have seen a marked improvement after this application.

Bee Stings, Bug Bites, Ticks:

I have applied 2 drops of *Purification* directly on the sting or bug bite followed by layering *Lavender* three times a day or more, as needed. *Geranium* is also wonderful for bee stings. It will take the swelling and sting out.

After being out and about adventuring through the woods behind our house, sometimes the cats come home with tiny, little backpackers… ticks. To solve this problem I first apply *Purification* or *Thieves* to the tick to get it to back out of the cat's skin. Then I rub in a bit of *Purification* to the entry spot to help prevent infection.

Depression/Grieving:

When a cat loses a loved one they can go through a period of mourning. I've found it's best to give them some space, cuddle when they want to and then maybe bring in another friend. When that hasn't worked then I have applied *Hope* on their paws and *Joy* on their heart. Just to offer a bit of support during this time of sadness.

Diarrhea:

I had a homeless cat dropped off at my boarding kennel years ago. He was very emaciated and when he finally got some meat on his bones, he had chronic diarrhea.

I started him on *Life 5* to re-colonize his intestinal tract. That did not do the trick alone. I suspect he may have had Giardia, so I started him on half water, half Silver Water/Colloidal Silver. We added this to his water dish and his stools firmed up. Then I began using *Life 5* again.

Ear Cankers:

Ear Cankers in cats are highly contagious and uncomfortable. I have treated this with one drop of *Chamomile* and *Lavender* in a teaspoon of warm olive oil. I put a small amount in the ear and massage it in thoroughly. As a supplement I also added the Silver Water to their drinking water.

Injury:

I assisted with a cat that was shot with a pellet gun. The pellet was lodged by it's spine and the cat had lost the ability to use it's hind legs. A willing veterinarian allowed the owner to apply the oils. He was sure the cat wouldn't make it so there was nothing to lose.

I want to add here, that if I had to use a "hotter" oil such as *Thyme, Lemongrass, Oregano, Cinnamon, Clove* or *Thieves,* I would be sure to dilute these oils with olive or coconut oil. Cats have very thin skin and the hotter oils can actually burn them.

We began the treatment by applying the oils *Helicrysum, Juniper* and *Cypress.* The owner continued to apply these oils diligently and the cat slowly recovered. His recovery may have been slow, but it was so good, that he was able to walk the top of the fence and escape the yard!

Another oil treatment I may have used for a situation like this would be one or two drops each of *Ledum, Geranium, PanAway* and *Ortho Sport* dripped along the cat's spine.

Testimonial

When my 19 year old cat, Trouble became constipated at the end of June, I wasn't too worried at first. He's had this problem before and it usually clears up within 24 hours. This time was different. he still hadn't used the litter box after 4 days, wouldn't eat and was hardly drinking anything. He was just laying on my bed and was very lethargic. I was afraid he was going to die, so I looked in Dr. Pitcairn's book on holistic animal medicine and it said to squirt a syringe full of warm water up his rear, so I did that. On the 5th day he was no better. In fact he was worse. The warm water hadn't done a thing to free his bowels.

That's when I started thinking about what oils I had and what might help Trouble. The first thing I grabbed was my bottle of Purification. I massaged a drop onto one ear (just the tops, not down the ear canal) and then a drop onto the other ear. I did not dilute the oil. Then I got my Ningxia Red Juice out of the refrigerator and tried to figure out how much to give a cat that only weighed about 10 pounds. I decided on a capful. So I filled the cap up and then put the juice into a syringe and squirted it down his throat. A few hours later, I put more purification on his ears and squirted more Ningxia Red Juice down his throat before going to bed. When I woke up in the morning, Trouble was no longer constipated. Although he was no longer blocked and ate up some food, he still wasn't acting like himself. So I put more Purification on his ear and squirted more Ningxia Red Juice down his throat.

When I got home from work, Trouble was still lying on my bed, but he was much more alert. His eyes were bright and his head was up. He was acting like he owned my bed and demanded to be fed that instant. I put more Purification on his ears and instead of squirting the Ningxia Red Juice down his throat, I mixed it into his canned food. He ate like he hadn't eaten in a month.

I put the Purification on his ears and the Ningxia Red Juice in his food again the next morning. A few days later, when I got home from work Trouble met me at the front door, demanding to be fed immediately if not sooner. After that I just put the Purification on his ears once a day for a week but kept putting the Ningxia Red Juice in his canned food. Since I spoiled him and fed him on my bed when he was so sick, once he was feeling better, Trouble still expected to be treated like royalty and fed on my bed. Even though he has "Kitty TV" when he eats (the windowsill I feed him on looks out at the young oak tree in my yard and he likes to watch the birds play while he eats) he still wanted to be fed on my bed. I had to pick him up and carry him to the windowsill that I put his food on. We went through that twice a day for a week until I finally convinced him that he was no longer going to be fed in my bed.

Now he loves the Ningxia Red Juice so much that unless I open a can of food (which he would like me to do several times a day) and add the Ningxia Red Juice to it, he won't eat it. Although I don't use the Purification on him every day any more, I still use it at least once a week. The difference in this cat is amazing. Two months later he is a totally different cat. He hadn't run through the house in quite awhile, but has been doing it for the last several days. He hasn't jumped up on anything in quite a while either, but this morning when I fed him, Trouble half climbed, half jumped on to the top of kitty condo so he could supervise me fixing his food. Instead of sleeping in my bed all the time when I'm home, he's sleeping on one of the couch pillows. He's living up to his name quite a bit now. The other day, he got up on my desk and preceded to knock a bunch of papers and other stuff to the floor several times. Yesterday he was swatting a ball around in my bathroom.

He's always been a very vocal cat and loves the sound of his own voice. Now he's even more vocal. He meets me at the front door when I come home from work, shopping or birding and demands to be fed, no matter what time it is. I feed him in the morning when I get up and at 5 pm every day unless I work late. He's also very demanding. When he wants to go to bed (he sleeps in my bed) he demands that I shut the computer and TV off and go to bed. When he wants me to get up in the morning, even if I don't have to be up early, he walks on me and loudly demands that I get up to feed him. It's like the Purification and Ningxia Red Juice are reversing the aging process because Trouble's starting to act more and more like he did when he was much younger. He'll be 20 in April and if I keep giving him the Ningxia Red Juice and putting the Purification on his ears, I expect him to live for many more years.

I am 100% sure that if it wasn't for the Purification and Ningxia Red Juice, Trouble might have died before I could get him to a vet. He's a typical male cat/child and can be a real pain in the butt, but I love him very much and wouldn't have him any other way, except in the middle of the night.

Kim, Merritt Island, FL

Parasites:

I've used the *Ningxia Red Juice* for years with cats, mixing in a couple drops of oil or *Mineral Essence*.

Worming can be accomplished with the same disguise. I have poked a hole in the *ParaFree* capsule and dropped 2 or 3 drops in a small amount of *Ningxia Red Juice* and squirted it into the back of the cat's mouth, using a syringe. They won't thank you for it but it does help things go down easier. I also have an applicator that allows me to suction the wormer liquid in and then administer to the cat, even when the cat is sure I can't get a thing between its teeth!

When I've had to handle an argumentative cat, I wrapped it in a towel to save myself from getting scratched.

I have also applied a drop or 2 of *DiGize* on the cat's tummy. Some cats are pretty agreeable, others won't appreciate it at all but it needs to be done.

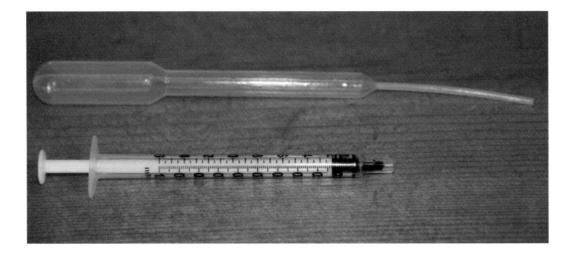

Passing Away:

When I have assisted my cats in crossing the Rainbow Bridge I apply *Peace and Calming* to their paws to help them feel more peaceful and relaxed during what can be a very stressful time. Applying *Joy* and *Transformation* to their heart and head can also be beneficial.

Poisoning:

Our cat Dozer is a healthy 11 year old cat. He has been raised with Young Living products in our home since he was a little rescue kitten.

He's an important member of our family, but days in our house can get wildly busy and sometimes something can be over-looked. That happened to Dozer a couple years ago.

I noticed he was asleep on our bathroom floor one day. He was back there that night and the next day but I didn't give it a second thought. We all continued on with our busy schedules. What I didn't notice, was that it wasn't that he was back in that spot, it was that he had never left that spot. By the next night, it dawned on me that he might be ill! I asked if anyone had seen him moving around the house and nobody had. So he hadn't eaten or gotten anything to drink nor had he used his litter box. I went to him to wake him up and he barely responded.

I went and got my syringe, 1 Tablespoon of Ningxia Red and 3 drops of Mineral Essence, sucked it up and force fed this mixture to him. He didn't argue. We brought water and a litter box and put it near him in our bathroom, so he wouldn't have to move much. I've seen symptoms like this before in a cat and in that case the cat had been poisoned. We suspected he'd eaten a mouse that had eaten poison. Death can happen pretty swiftly and we knew we could lose him. I gave him two more doses before I went to bed around midnight. By the next morning he was up and drinking water. I gave him 3 more doses throughout the day and by evening he was eating canned cat food and had used his litter box. By the following day you would never have guessed he'd been so close to death at all!

We were so fortunate to have a way to help Dozer recover so quickly and have since helped an 8 week old kitten recover with the same mixture but feeding less at a time. I always have Ningxia Red and Mineral Essence in my refrigerator! I have used it with all my animals at one time or another!

Urinary Tract Infections:

I have had a few cats come down with Urinary Tract Infections (UTI's). To battle these I have added *K & B* supplement to their food. I also massaged two to five drops of *Inspiration* or *Juniper, Ledum* or *Geranium* over the kidney area. I have done this once a day until the UTI was cleared up.

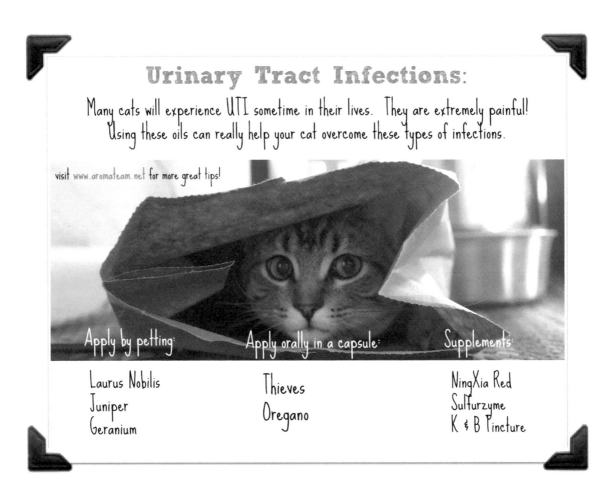

Vomiting:

One of my customers had an elderly cat that vomited daily. She didn't want tests run at his advanced age, she just wanted him to be more comfortable. She tried the usual diet change and worming, but there was no change.

I gave her some *DiGize* and she rubbed two or three drops on his belly daily. The vomiting slowed down to once every two or three weeks. He was more comfortable, gained some of his weight back and lived another year and a half.

Wounds, Cuts, Abrasions:

Sometimes cats get into fights. When my cats have come home beat up I begin their treatment by gently bathing the injured area before layering the oils on. I have applied *Thieves* or *Lavender Foaming Hand Soap* to the wound. You may want to have a helper when doing this with a cat.

To make this experience a bit easier I have simply combined the oils I wanted to use with a bit of water in a spray bottle, shook it well and sprayed it on the wound. The oils I've used are *Melrose*, *Helichrysum*, *Lavender* and *Purification*.

Section Three

Horses

"For every drug that benefits a patient,
there is a natural substance that can achieve the same effect."

-Dr Carl C. Pfeiffer

I have worked with a lot of horses and have found that it doesn't take large amounts of the oils or supplements to be effective. Most horses are fed natural diets free from the preservatives and additives in dog and cat food. Because of this their bodies are much less polluted than those of dogs, cats and even humans. They respond very quickly to small amounts of the oils and supplements.

Remember that any oil is better than no oil! There are so many constituents in each oil, even the single oils, that any one oil will probably do more than what is written about it. Sometimes it's the oil that doesn't immediately come to mind that does the most good!

Flip through the dog section, too, as some of the things discussed will help in horse emergencies as well.

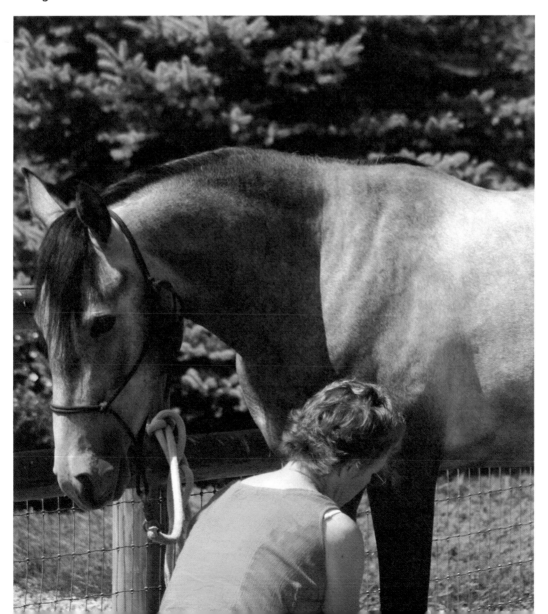

Abscesses:

I have applied *Melaleuca* or *Melrose* to an abscess, covered by a hot towel, in order to get the abscess to come to a head and begin draining. After it's been broken open and is starting to drain I have used a syringe, with the needle removed, and squirted *Melrose* or *Lavender* directly into the abscess, flushing it. Afterwards I would cover the wound with *Animal Scents Ointment* to seal and protect it.

If you don't have any of those oils and catch the abscess early enough you can use *Ortho Sport*, applying it liberally to the abscess area. *Ortho Sport* doesn't get too hot because it is already mixed with mixing oils.

Horses can also get abscesses in their hooves. I have worked with this situation on a horse that we didn't want to boot so we applied *Thieves* to the abscess area, even using a syringe with the needle on, to get the *Thieves* right into the abscess hole. I sucked the *Thieves* into the syringe by inserting the needle directly into the bottle. The next day it was much better. We reapplied the *Thieves* and the abscess healed beautifully.

Asthma/Heaves:

I worked with one horse that had a chronic cough. He had a very difficult time getting enough air, really working to suck in his breath. These symptoms point to the horse having Heaves, symptoms similar to asthma in humans. His cough had been going on for a number of years, though the cough became much worse in the fall. The owner thought it was either allergies or induced by the cooler air. Over the years the vet was called in at these times and gave the horse an injection to soothe the coughing.

The owner and I worked together and changed up his diet, replacing his hay with hay cubes. We began his regiment with twelve drops of *RC* and *Raven* on his lung area, seven drops of *Citrus Fresh* on his belly, seven drops of *Lemon* down the underside of his neck and four more drops of *RC* layered over the *Lemon* on his neck.

With all the coughing he was doing we felt he must have had a sore throat. So we also added nine drops of *Longevity* to his grain.

We only did this regiment once a day for two weeks, then we gradually cut down on the amount of oils used over the next two weeks, as the horse improved. It took two months for all his symptoms to disappear.

He remains on a maintenance program of two drops of *Longevity* added topically to his grain. Twice a week he gets six drops of *Lemon* on his neck. We started him on loose hay again and his symptoms have not returned!

Testimonial

I had a four month old colt December of 2008, that had developed a breathing problem. In talking to the vet, we were not sure if it was an allergy or just a dusty hay problem. I used R.C., Thieves and Oregano in steaming water. We put a towel over his nose and he lowered his head right into the bucket. He stayed there as long as he needed it. We only had to use this treatment three times. He cleared up within three days.

About three weeks ago, I had a three year old mare that scraped her leg. Her knee swelled up so much that it was three times it's normal size. I used Purification, then Thieves and Peppermint (all diluted in olive oil). I wrapped the entire leg with vet wrap so the heat would help the oils penetrate faster. Within 24 hours the leg reduced to half the size. I repeated it for two more days and the swelling was completely gone! The scrape on her leg is healing great. And the best thing I have noticed in using the oils is, no granular tissue aka proud flesh ever grows in the wound!

Tabitha

Botulism:

I worked with two mares that were in severe distress. They had to be moved into the barn using a tractor, because they could not use their hind legs when they were found. When I saw them, they were both standing, but had to lean against the walls of the stall. One wouldn't eat anything, the other wouldn't drink. They were mother and daughter, both adult mares. The mother was 24, I don't recall the age of the younger mare, though she was pregnant.

These two were always together, companions in everything, including eating. It was apparent that they had ingested something, most likely it was hidden in the hay they shared.

I did an assessment and thought it was likely the foal was dead, but because the mare was exhibiting nerve damage in her spine, she wasn't able to pass it. Her hind end wasn't working properly.

I began their treatment with a *Raindrop Technique* (see page 85). One for each mare. Then, I put twelve drops of *Peppermint* and twelve drops of *DiGize* on each of their belly's. Next, I massaged Neurogen Cream into their backs from mid spine down to the dock of their tails, just as you would do with a human dealing with paralysis.

Now I would mix two Tablespoons *Mineral Essence*, thirteen drops *Juniper*, twenty drops *Copaiba*, nineteen drops *Laurus Nobilis* and fourteen drops *Peppermint*. These oils are wonderful for nerve damage issues. The amount will vary depending on size of the animal and area in need. Drip this mixture onto the spine and massage in.

I put two drops of *DiGize* inside their lower lips, then I mixed *Thieves* with water and squirted the mixture into their mouths using a syringe without a needle. Lastly, I gave them each five ounces of Colloidal Silver orally.

We spent some time observing them after this treatment. The one who wasn't interesting in eating, started eating. The one that wouldn't drink began drinking.

I went back two days later and repeated the above treatment. That was all the ranch manager wanted as this was all new to him. In the end the older mare passed away. The younger mare lived. She did pass the still born foal a couple of weeks later as her nerves started to work again. She did get the feeling and function of her hind end back.

If they had been mine, I would have treated them every day. As it was I was pleased that one survived. Botulism is very deadly and difficult to fight.

Calming:

I worked at a ranch with numerous stallions. Several of them were in need of treatments. One was particularly angry, aggressive and high strung. He had offered to attack several of the stable workers when they entered his pen. The first time he was brought to me, he knocked the stable girl down and came straight to me, searching for the oils he smelled. As I applied his oils, he stood beautifully for me.

I started with *Peace and Calming* on his nose, ears, on his heart and on his knees, so when he would lower his head he would smell the oil. I then went on to apply the oils for his digestive system. He calmly walked out when I was through. I oiled him twice a week. After the first couple of times he was noticeably more calm. He had calmed down so much that we didn't even need a halter to catch him. We just entered his pasture and he would meet us for his oiling.

I have also used *Gentle Baby* in the same way. All you need is one or two drops applied to the nose, ears, heart and knees.

There have been times that I couldn't get close enough to the horse to apply the calming oils, in that case I simply applied them to myself, on my hands, then running them through my hair. Horses will often offer to smell your hands and hair when they meet you and will benefit from the aromatherapy of the *Peace and Calming* or *Gentle Baby*. If the horse is very skeptical of me I will squat down, making myself smaller. This will bring up the horse's curiosity and they come over to check me out, again, inhaling the oils that I'm wearing.

When I have had to work on horses that are very fearful and may hurt me in their panic, I have started a session by diffusing *Peace and Calming*, *Chivalry* or *Gentle Baby* straight into their stall. You can also mist them with a spray bottle of oils mixed with water if you can't get close. Get creative!

Colds:

When I was called in for a horse with a cold I started the treatment with a *Raindrop Technique* (see page 85). I also applied twelve drops of *RC* and *Raven* on it's chest and lung area. I have also used *Longevity* mixed with a small amount of olive oil in a syringe and squirted it into the horse's mouth, once a day.

I have battled colds in my horses by applying twelve drops of *Longevity* or *Thieves* on the spine once a day as well. I did dilute with olive oil because these oils can get hot. If the horse is going to be out to pasture, under the sun, then you can apply these oils to the belly, diluting with the olive oil. The oils can react to the sun and get a little hotter than normal. I've found the horses enjoy the heat on their spine in the winter, however.

I have also diffused *Thieves*, *RC* or *Raven* for a couple of hours once or twice a day in the horse's stall if they are in a barn.

Colic:

I had a miniature horse that would colic easily. I have gained a great deal of experience with colic while helping this mare, as I treated her six times in one year, as well as the others I have helped since. I have been able to turn colic around in as little as twenty five minutes, though sometimes it can take as long as an hour and half, so don't give up!

I would treat a large horse exactly the same as I did the miniature horse, using the same amount of oils. Below is the regiment I followed when I treated her for the first time.

At 5:30 in the evening I noticed one of my mares, down, rolling and in obvious distress. This was my first time treating, what I suspected, was impaction colic. I believe she was impacted from overeating oats the night before. I knew this was a severe case of colic and we were losing ground fast with the mare.

We tried to keep her as quiet as possible, no walking and no rolling. I called eight veterinarians in a 250 mile radius and not one was home. It was on me, my son, my friend and the oils.

I began by layering ten drops each of *Peppermint* and *DiGize* on her belly every fifteen minutes. I put four drops of *Peppermint*, mixed it in water, then sucked it up in a syringe and gave it to her orally. Some fell out, so I rubbed the mister on her tongue and gums. I mixed four drops of *DiGize* in water, again sucked it up into a syringe and applied it rectally.

I was doing everything I could think of to save my mare. And yet she was looking worse and worse. I applied *DiGize* on the coronet band of her hooves and vita flexed it in, rubbed it down the front of the hoof and then applied some to the bottom of her hooves as well.

I used *Valor* on her frogs as well, then put *Peace and Calming* on her belly and Joy on the crease of her throat where her head and neck join.

I spent a lot of time massaging her stomach while she was laying down. Her pain was intense for a long time. At one point I felt she was getting ready to give up. But I never gave up on her!

Finally at about 9:30 that night, she rolled up from laying on her side, propped herself up on her chest and perked her ears up, looking around with interest. It was soon after that she stood up, shook herself and busied herself with her baby. She looked great!

She had been marinated from the inside out and once again… the oils saved a life!

I now put twelve drops of *Peppermint* and *DiGize* on the umbilical area every fifteen minutes, for about four applications. I pour about three to four cups of water into a bowl, then add twenty drops of *Peppermint*, twenty drops of *DiGize* and six to ten *Detoxyme Capsules*, opened and sprinkled into the water/oil mixture. I then mix it well and suck it up into a syringe so I can apply it orally and also suck it up with my turkey baster and administer it rectally.

I do this every five to ten minutes until I have squirted the mixture in both ends, four times. Then I take a break for about half an hour. I observe the horse and just apply oils topically to the stomach. Usually I repeat the internal application one or two more times, or until the horse is back to normal.

I walk them a bit after awhile but in the beginning I just have them standing. So far, every time, they loosen up and are able to pass manure after this regiment. Sometimes it's diarrhea first and then will firm up. Sometimes the first manure passed is very dry and crumbly. Once they begin going to the bathroom, they perk up quickly. After they have recovered they will often object to having me near their butt for a bit… they are fine and will forgive me after a few days!

I have also helped horses on trail rides that have shown signs of gas colic. For this I applied twelve drops of *DiGize* and *Peppermint* to the belly, rubbing it in. I reapplied these two oils, every fifteen minutes and kept the horse walking. I have had the pain stop, the gas released and the horse back to normal, ready to ride in less than thirty minutes. I had the owner wait an extra hour before riding back down the trail and take it slow, but the horse was recovered and happy. He smelled good too!

Disinfecting Horse Brushes:

Disinfecting Horse Brushes:

Simply drop a few drops of Purification Essential Oil into a bucket of warm water and allow your brushes to soak for 10 minutes. Then wipe dry with a clean rag. You can also fill a cap full of the Thieves Household cleaner, pour into a spray bottle, fill with water and shake up the mixture. Then spray your brushes down and let them sit for a few minutes, after which you wipe the wood dry with a clean rag.

please visit www.theessentialhorse.com for more great tips!

either a few drops of this in a bucket...

or spray with this!

Falls/Trauma:

Horses can fall when riding in a horse trailer, when unloading from the trailer and also while on trail rides. When this has happened and I've been there, I applied *Trauma Life* to the muzzle and generously applied *Ortho Sport* to the legs and spine. I don't go on rides without it and also keep some in my horse trailer.

Flies/Fly Spray:

I've come up with several different natural fly sprays but this is the latest and greatest!

In a 24-ounce spray bottle mix one Tablespoon of *Thieves Household Cleaner*, ten drops of *Purification*, fifteen drops of *Citronella*, seven drops of *Idaho Tansy* and seven drops of *Peppermint*. Fill the rest of the bottle with water, shake well and spray on your horse!

You may have to respray the horse after working up a sweat. The oils will be so great for your horse's hair coat!

Founder/Laminitis:

When I have helped horses who are suffering from founder, either from eating too much green grass or resulting in some stress in their environment, I start by adding four capsules of *Detoxzyme* in a small amount of water, which I apply orally with a syringe, daily.

For immediate relief of hoof pain and to increase circulation I use six drops of *Cypress* around the coronet band of each hoof, then I use six drops of *PanAway*, *White Fir* or *Helicrysum* around the coronet band of each hoof.

I then drop twelve to sixteen drops of *Peppermint* on the hoof wall and rub in to help cool the hoof. A foundered hoof is very hot from inflammation. Next, I put six drops of *Peppermint* and *PanAway* on the frog of each hoof. I did this once a day for several days with one pony that I rehabilitated. With another that was more severe I applied this twice a day. *Valor* dripped down the spine will help with any discomfort caused by a change of posture from carrying themselves differently due to the pain of the founder. They are trying to walk carefully and can throw out their backs and hips.

Twelve to sixteen drops of *Valor* down the spine can help realign their body. They don't call *Valor* a "chiropractor in a bottle" for nothing!

Working with a good farrier afterwards, to help keep the feet trimmed properly, is very important.

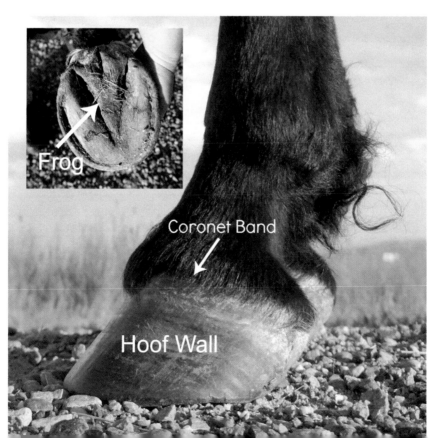

Hoof Infections:

I have dealt with different things such as abscesses and thrush. Both are tricky and having the support of a good vet is important. Especially for the abscesses as they usually need to be opened and drained in order for healing to happen.

I helped one horse that had stepped on a nail and another that had an abscess. To support healing I used *Melaleuca* or *Thieves*, neat, in a syringe with the needle, so I could be very exact in getting the oil into the abscess. Then I booted the hoof to help keep it clean and bacteria free.

I also had the owners soak the hoof in warm water with Epsom salts, fifteen drops of *Lavender* and fifteen drops of *Melrose* or *Melaleuca* to help draw out the abscess and to avoid an abscess in the hoof that had a nail in it. After the soaking, I applied *Thieves*, neat to the hoof, then covered that with *Animal Scents Ointment* and booted the hoof to help protect it.

When I've helped with thrush I like to use either *Melrose* or *Australian Blue*. I apply twelve drops of either oil, neat, to the bottom of the hoof twice daily.

Immune System- Weak:

I helped my sister with a weakened three day old miniature horse foal. He was having a hard time getting started, weak and not nursing well. I had her start using *Longevity* on his belly, near the umbilical area and also supplement him with one teaspoon of *Ningxia Red Juice* and pinch of *Sulfurzyme*, using a syringe, orally, once a day. Too much *Sulfurzyme* (even just 1/4 of a teaspoon) gave the foal diarrhea, but she could just use a pinch. The foal perked up!

I have also worked with larger horses who are suffering from weakened immune systems, by adding two Tablespoons of *Ningxia Red Juice* and one teaspoon of *Sulfurzyme* to the grain ration. I have also applied six to twelve drops of *Longevity* along the spine, massaging it in with a small amount of olive oil.

I have used the *Raindrop Technique* (see page 85) for raising the immune system as well, with great success. This works especially well before or after horses get their vaccinations.

Testimonial

My young North American Curly Horse was due to have his vaccines. I don't usually give vaccinations, but I was boarding him at a boarding barn and wanted to be sure he was covered just in case. You sometimes can't be sure of the health of the other horses at the barn and they come and go quite a lot, so just felt I should cover all my bases.

He had his first go round and was going to need a boost of the strangles vaccine, but the vaccinations themselves made my poor Billy sick. He had goopy eyes, a dry cough and his guttural pouches got very firm and hot. He was clearly uncomfortable, which also caused him to be irritable. We had to postpone the strangles booster until he became well. It took several weeks, with the help of the oils (Thieves and Peppermint) both in his food and applied topically he began feeling better. BUT he still needed that booster and I knew he would have a similar reaction.

So I called my Aunt Sara and asked her to come do a Raindrop Technique before the strangles booster. I thought the Raindrop would boost his immune system and help him fight off the reaction to the vaccine.

He loved the raindrop, showing us by making funny faces and standing so nicely. Just like a gentleman.

And a few days later when he was boosted with the strangles vaccine, he didn't have any nasty side effects at all! He stayed healthy as a horse!

Mindy   Ennis, MT

Lacerations:

I have treated many lacerations. One treatment I've used with great success is mix six to eight drops of *Helichrysum* with a bit of water and using a syringe, squirt it into the wound, rinsing it out. Then squirt six drops of *Purification* mixed with a bit of water into the wound. Lastly, cover the wound with some *Animal Scents Ointment*.

I have also used *Melaleuca*, neat, on the wound, with no scaring or hair color change.

Ortho Sport has worked wonderfully on wounds around the pastern/fetlock area. Some wounds located around the fetlock can be deeper than first thought and can get very swollen, causing lameness. The *Ortho Sport* works wonders both as a topical treatment and helps with swelling.

Leg Injuries

Bone Chips:

I have helped people deal with bone chips by layering three drops of *PanAway*, along with three drops of *Wintergreen* over the area of the bone chip two times a day for a week, then giving the area four days off. Then again layering the oils over the area. If the skin shows signs of drying out, then apply some coconut oil to the area to help moisturize the skin.

Ligaments/Tendons Injuries:

I have treated torn ligaments and tendons by layering *Lemongrass* and *PanAway* over the injury. I also added one teaspoon *BLM powder* and *Sulfurzyme* topically to their grain, once a day.

Cut or Severed Tendon:

When my sister's horse cut his tendon while out to pasture, it wasn't noticed for a day. They were devastated when they discovered the injury. She called me right away and began a treatment plan. First I had her wash the wound with *Lavender* mixed with some warm water. Then she added six drops of *Tsuga* straight into the wound, six drops of *Melrose* and three drops of *Helicrysm*. After the wound was packed with *Animal Scents Ointment* she dropped four drops of *White Fir* around the wounded area to help with swelling. She then wrapped the area. She treated the wound daily for three weeks. It took six months to heal, but it healed sound.

Soon after this injury, my niece's horse severed her deep digital flexor tendon in her hind leg. It was noticed immediately and the vet was called. While waiting for the vet to arrive she applied the oils, *Melrose* and *Tsuga* directly into the wound. The vet sutured the tendon and the mare's leg was put in a cast. My niece dropped the oils down into the cast daily and in six weeks, when the cast was removed, the wound had healed up beautifully, without scarring or scar tissue. The mare went on to be 100% sound.

Melanoma:

Melanoma is more common in gray horses. I was first introduced to it at a Paso Fino ranch when I first went to show them how to work with the oils. The mare had been getting slowly, but progressively worse over the last couple of years. When she was brought before me she had some large tumors around her head and neck and many down her tail. She was very lethargic because she couldn't lie down. It was too hard for her to get up. Arthritis was also a problem. She had been dragging her hind hooves and would pivot when turning so she didn't have to lift them. I also noticed she never swished her tail.

The first thing I did was a *Raindrop Technique* (see page 85), then I applied *Longevity*, *Orange*, *Frankincense* and *Lavender* on each tumor. As I worked on her she started lifting her hind legs as though the feeling was coming back to them. The owner was very surprised because she hadn't really been able to move her hind legs for nearly two years. She then began swishing her tail! I was called the next day and told the mare had lain down the night before to sleep. They couldn't remember seeing her lay down for at least the last year. I was hired that day!

We applied oils twice a week and saw her energy and comfort increase, so that she even started to run in the pasture again. The tumor growth slowed, though they did not recede. She continues to do well, is active and they can even ride her again!

Ovarian Tumor:

Testimonial

I rode dressage and did a lot of studying, practicing, taking lessons and attending clinics. I hauled Abby all over the valley where we lived and hours away to ride in the mountains, trail riding by ourselves and with others. Abby was always very laid back and easy going whether we were alone or with a group of horses. She got along with everyone.

Until one summer when my normally sweet mare turned into a raging wild thing! She began attacking other horses and then turned that rage on me, ears pinned, teeth bared. Quickly I decided to get her to the vet to see what was going on. Was she in pain? What the heck was happening? She was unrideable.

The vet started with some blood tests which showed high levels of testosterone in her system. Her levels were twice what a stallion would have during the height of breeding season. After doing an ultrasound the vet found a grapefruit sized tumor on one of her ovaries. This was the root of all the aggressive behavior.

The tumor was so large that the vet was going to have to remove it through her flank. They would have to take the tumor and the ovary. This was going to be a major surgery. We scheduled it for a week from her diagnosis.

My Aunt Sara called me during this week long wait and asked if Abby and I would help her make a video about applying the oils to animals. She had the dog and the cat, but needed a horse and a nice barn setting to film in. I agreed after telling her how dangerous Abby had become because of her tumor. Aunt Sara said we would use a lot of Peace and Calming and hope that that would help Abby relax. Sounded good to me! I needed a lot of Peace and Calming myself to help me deal with all the stress I had been feeling over the tumor!

I found a barn that would allow us to film and we went ahead with the project.

We had a wonderful time making the DVD (Essential Tips for Healthy Pets). There was lots of laughter and silliness and through it all Abby only tried to bite, paw and kick at us a tiny bit. After applying what felt like a bottle of Peace and Calming to her knees and chest (and allowing her to smell and taste it) we were able to get on with the show!

When I took Abby back to the vet for her surgery he wanted to do another ultra sound to check on the size of the tumor, to be sure it hadn't gotten any larger.

Instead what he found was that it was gone. GONE. Vanished, without a trace. He was stunned. He said he had never witnessed a tumor of that size just disappearing! He asked what I did and I told him about the oils and the DVD that my Aunt and I had done. He was absolutely wowed and told me to keep up the good work!

Abby walked out of there with a clean bill of health. Years ago I sold her to a great home where she foaled a few lovely foals and gave her new owner's kids riding lessons. She is now 20 years old and is retired from breeding, but still living a healthy, happy life!

Amazing. Abby went on to live a full, active life, thanks to Young Living Essential Oils.

Mindy Ennis, MT

Skin:

I have helped horses with rain rot by using two ounces of *Animal Scents Shampoo* mixed with twenty drops of *Australian Blue*, ten drops of *Lavender* and five drops of *Ocotea*, shaken well and applied directly to the rain rot.

Skin Conditions

Animal Ointment is a soothing salve to be used topically on irritations, cuts and abrasions.

Put 3 drops of Geranium mixed with a carrier oil (coconut oil, avocado oil, olive oil) in your palm and activate by rubbing clockwise. Then apply to the hot spot on the skin. Cover with the Animal Ointment!

please visit www.theessentialhorse.com for more great tips!

Strangles:

I was called by a client to help with their horse that had contracted strangles. The vet had been called and treatment had begun. She wanted to support that treatment with the oils. To begin the oil treatment we applied twelve drops *Exodus II*, three drops *Melrose*, mixed with coconut oil to the abscesses. The owner did this two times a day for eleven days. After which we did a *Raindrop Technique* (see page 85) to help raise the immune system. The owner disinfected the horse's buckets and pen by putting *Thieves*, *Purification* and *Oregano* in a spray bottle, mixing it with water and spraying the area.

Transportation:

When I haul my horses I like to apply *Ortho Sport* to their spines and knees. Then I put two drops of *White Angelica* to their shoulders and two drops of *Peace and Calming* to the lower lip or heart area. If I can only do one of these, I always apply the *Ortho Sport*. I never travel without it.

Trauma:

I have worked on horses that have suffered all kinds of trauma from being neglected, to being physically abused at the hands of humans. When I help these horses I start by using *Trauma Life* on the nose and the outer edges of the ears and if I can a drop or two inside the lower lip. I will also apply six drops of *Peace and Calming* to the heart and three drops on each knee.

Another great treatment is a couple of drops of *White Angelica* on each shoulder along with the *Trauma Life* on the nose.

Remember, you don't have to use all of these oils. Even just one will be beneficial.

Twisted Gut:

My miniature horse stallion showed symptoms of having a twisted gut when I noticed him throwing himself down on the ground, rolling and rolling. I immediately took my oiling kit out to the barnyard and began treatment. I mixed twenty four drops of *Peppermint* and *DiGize*, six drops of *Detoxzyme* with a little water. I then administered the mixture both orally, with a syringe and rectally, with the baster every fifteen minutes. I was also applying twelve drops of *DiGize* and *Peppermint* to his tummy and four drops of each to the bottom of his hooves.

When he was still throwing himself down and trying to roll I decided to load him up and take him to the veterinarian, a two hour drive away. Apparently taking a ride in a trailer can help relax those muscles and things corrected themselves. He stood the whole way and by the time we got to the clinic he was fine!

The vet didn't know anything about oils and smugly said, "As soon as that Peppermint smell wears off, he'll be fine." I smugly replied that he'd best not bend over in front of me, as I may be armed with my baster!

Testimonial

A couple years ago a friend of mine who has a Welsh Pony that had been abused by a prior owner, participated in an oiling clinic that I was teaching. PJ's first owner would tie him up and then whip him...he had nowhere to go but forward, hitting the post he was tied to, which caused physical and emotional wounding. Kim purchased PJ and had been working with him to help him get over this trauma for quite some time.   Though his physical wounds had healed, the emotional trauma was more difficult to overcome. He had trust issues and was taking out his anger and frustration about human interactions on the other horses in the pasture, bullying them during feed time, constantly chasing them away from the hay.

I had his owner just reach in and pick out oils from all the oils I had at the clinic and then apply them to her pony, PJ.

The energetically chosen oils she picked out to use on him were:

- Transformation applied in his mouth
- Geranium applied behind his poll
- Sacred Mountain applied on his poll
- Western Red Cedar applied on chest
- Jasmine applied on lower neck
- Eucalyptus Globulous applied on upper part of chest
- Eucalyptus Radiata applied on upper part of neck
- Valarian applied on the back of both cheeks

It was fascinating to watch him as Kim applied the oils one by one.   He started out with his head high and tense, but within moments of licking the Transformation he started to relax and be curious. By the time the Valarian went on his cheeks he was completely relaxed, head down, allowing Kim to stand right in front of him with a hand on each cheek. In watching this exchange, it was obvious by the look on Kim's face, that she had never been able to touch him like that. He would never allow himself to be in such a vulnerable spot, yet here he was enjoying it! She put him back in his stall and he was very relaxed. She reported that when she let him out to eat with the others that evening, he quietly went and ate without trying to boss anyone away! As with the first oil he tasted, he was Transformed!

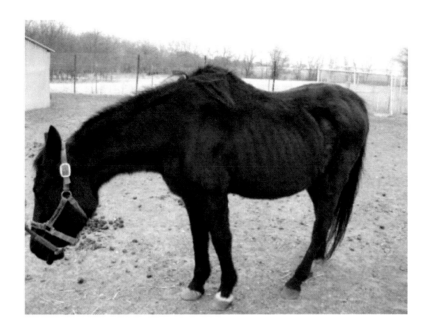

Testimonial

In January of 2009, I was asked by a lady that I know to come and give the last of her Silkie chickens a forever home. I said fine and was on my way. A year prior to this, her husband had passed and she was left with animals and a place that she did not know how to take care of. When I got there I realized one of the animals was a lovely old Polish Arabian gelding. He stood in a dry lot looking like he needed a place to die. He was about to turn 20 years old and had been the victim of someone not knowing how to take care of a horse. Before we discussed the chickens I asked her what she was going to do with him. She said she was waiting to hear back from the SPCA but she had been waiting for quite awhile. I told her that I would give him a home.

We returned in a couple of days with our trailer behind our truck to pick the poor guy up. His name is Rhythm. This is a picture of him at the time.

He doesn't look as bad as he was because his coat was very long, covering how thin he was.

Of course our first venture was to see a vet to be sure I wasn't bringing home any health problems that would put my own horses at risk. The vet said he might just need food and for me to take him home and try to give him his life back.

So I did.

One of the first things I knew to do for him was to contact Candace Hoke to have a Zyto Compass done on him to see what Young Living Essentail Oils and treatments needed to be done on him. We found that we needed to use a lot of the healing oils along with the oils to help with attitude/emotions. I remember using Exodus II, Egyptian Gold, Melrose, Sara, Christmas Spirit, Thieves, Lavender, Peppermint and several others. I put them on his head and some at the base of his nose. He started turning around but did suffer from all kinds of other old horse problems. So I soon started putting a blend of the oils mentioned above as well as Thieves Household Cleaner in his food. This combination of oils kept me from having to let him live on antibiotics, which he obviously couldn't tolerate, for a chronic sinus infection from teeth that had to be pulled and a scare we had with Pigeon fever.

During this period of time, which encompassed several years, I was fortunate enough to go to a wonderful clinic on carrying for animals with YLEO's that was put on by Sara Kenney. Not only did I learn a lot from her there, but she is the kind of person you can follow up with afterwards. So Sara and I did a lot of brain storming, figuring out how to help this old gentleman. And I know that had a lot to do with his recovery. I will always be grateful for all of her input on how to do what we were trying to get done.

This horse has been through the mill of things being wrong with him. Thanks to the YLEO's he has come out on top and is now getting ready to turn 25 years old. He is a certified therapy horse through a national organization and of course one of the sweetest and best horses I could ever imagine owning.

He now lives on a top quality feed, clean water, good hay and some awesome supplements.

This is my Rhythm today.

We call him "The Horse That Oils Built."

Raindrop Technique

The Raindrop Technique uses the oils to bring about balance and harmony, both to the body and the mind. I have found it to be beneficial for raising the immune system as well. It is a beautiful combination of oils that bring about a peaceful feeling for both the horses and the humans applying the Raindrop.

To begin, I use three to six drops of *Peace and Calming* or *Valor* on the nose, the heart and the knees.

Starting with the right front leg, the right front as seen when standing in front of the horse, you will apply the oils in a counterclockwise fashion, right front, right hind, left hind, left front. Apply six to eight drops of *Valor* to the heel bulbs of each hoof.

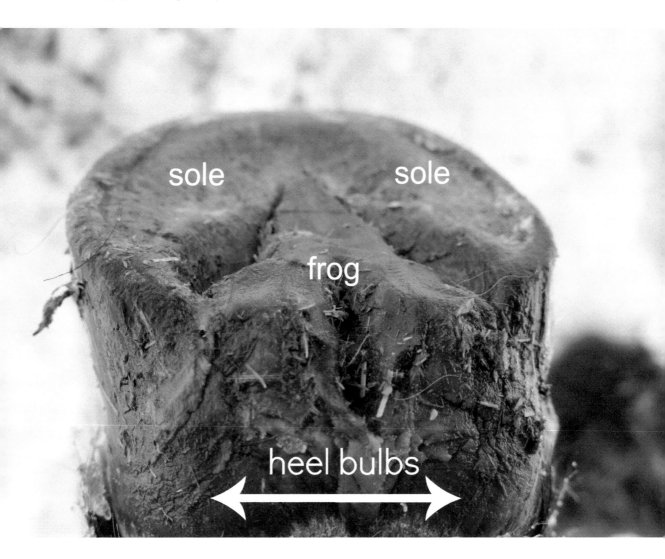

Then I put *Valor* on the point of the shoulder, at the base of the neck- the front part of the shoulders, and hold.

Then I move my hands to do a hold at the withers and the sacrum, which is just in front of the tail. It can help to have two people to manage the hold if you have a very large horse.

This next part also works very well if you have two people to apply the oils. One on the right side and one on the left. It is possible to do it alone, as well, it just takes more time.

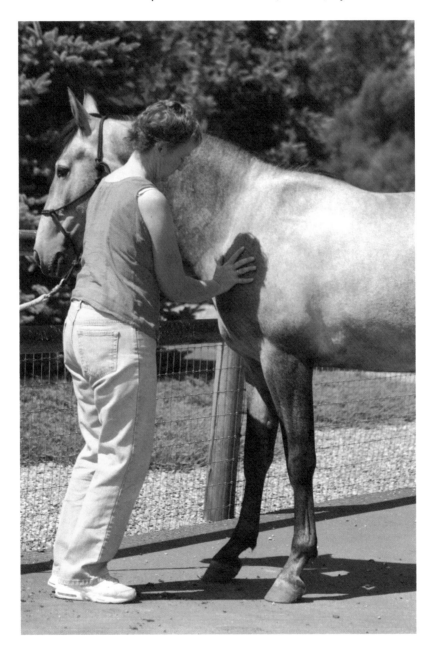

Apply *Oregano* and *Thyme* on the hind legs, around the coronet band and Vita Flex in the oils. Vita Flex is a simple massage technique. Using just the fingertips, apply a small amount of pressure and roll your fingers over onto the nail bed and back to the tips, moving your fingers along the coronet band. It's a rolling movement.

Then you will layer the following oils on from stifle to hoof, Vita Flexing after each oil:

- *Basil*
- *Cypress*
- *Marjoram*
- *Wintergreen*
- *Peppermint*

Next, apply these oils along the spine.
- *Oregano*
- *Thyme*
- *Basil*
- *Cypress*
- *Marjoram*
- *Wintergreen*
- *Peppermint*
- *Aroma Siez*

Hold the oils six inches above the spine, dropping them up the spine from tail to withers.

After each oil, massage it in using a small clockwise, circular motion, with both hands, then cat scratch it in. Then do long strokes, always going from tail to withers.

Repeat each technique three times.

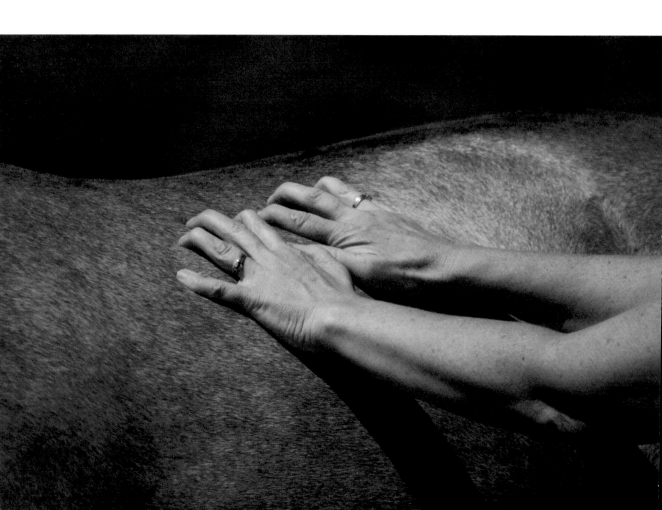

Next apply *Ortho Sport* and work it in for three to five minutes, first massaging it in using small clockwise circles, then cat scratching, then using the long strokes from tail to withers, then lastly, Vita Flex it in. Remember to always use both hands when massaging the oils in.

Then place a warm, wet towel on the horse's spine and cover it with a nice thick saddle pad or more, dry towels. This will drive the oils in deeper. Apply a bit of pressure, rubbing the spine through the towels and blanket. Leave the towel and blanket on for at least fifteen to twenty minutes.

To finish, stretch all four legs, starting with the right front and moving around the horse counterclockwise. Lift the leg, then straighten, gently pulling the leg to allow for a stretch. Only stretch as much as the horse is comfortable with.

Allow your horse to do some stretches of it's own at this time as well. Some will want to stretch their necks, they may yawn or lower their head to allow a nice stretch through the back. Your horse knows what it needs, so just allow some moving around at this time.

This treatment is fabulous for performance horses, helping boost the immune system, and for back and leg problems. Do you have a mysterious lameness issue? Try the Raindrop Technique.

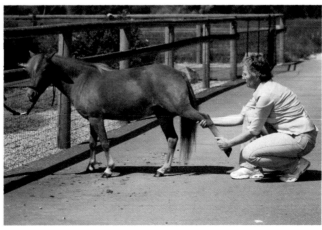

Diffusing Essential Oils for Animals

Many people have asked me if it is safe to diffuse essential oils around their pets, especially cats and birds. My answer will always be absolutely YES! As long as you are using Young Living Essential Oils. The pure quality of Young Living Oils enhances your pet's wellness in body, mind and spirit while impure essential oils will build up in their sensitive bodies and contribute to illness.

We diffuse oils in our house all the time and my dog and cat's don't mind at all.

Diffusing oils in a small room where you can close your pet in can come in handy when you have a dog with kennel cough or any of your pets have a respiratory issue.

When oils are diffused in a home, kennel or aviary, they purify the air by removing toxins and other harmful microscopic debris. They also increase the atmospheric oxygen of the air and boost levels of beneficial ozone and negative ions which dramatically inhibits the growth and reproduction of airborne pathogens.

Further, as the odorous molecules drift to the various surfaces of the room, they rapidly kill virtually all pathogenic bacteria, viruses, molds and fungi they come into contact with.

Many oils such as *Lemongrass, Orange, Grapefruit, Eucalyptus Globulus, Melaleuca Alternifolia, Lavender, Frankincense* and *Lemon* along with the blends *Thieves* and *Purification* are extremely effective for eliminating and destroying airborne germs and bacteria. I have brought my pets home from kennels and clinic and started the diffuser for them right away to help kill any germs, bacteria or virus they may have been exposed to.

I have friends that have created "diffusing tents" in barn stalls to treat respiratory issues for horses, calves and goats.

Testimonial

Hi Sara,
I was just reading your post about your new book, I can't wait until it comes out.

In your post you spoke of using the oils on a mallard duck. I have the little call ducks which are very similar to the mallard.

Can you tell me which oils I can use on them and the best way to use them? I have been wanting to use my oils on them but have been afraid of overwhelming them or harming them more. Also which ones that I can not use on them.

I have one little female in particular that I want to help (Missy). She stays in my house because she has something wrong, I am not sure if she has had a stroke or if it is from an injury. She has trouble walking sometimes, she has a writhing type motion when she turns her neck to the right. Lately she has been quacking and acting like she was startled, I am thinking there is some pain going on when she does this.

She has made her home under my spiral stairs in my living room. She really wants to be out with the others but they pick on her and I am afraid she is not strong enough to deal with them. She used to be with 2 of them when they hatched in august but when they went out to the pen with the others she had to stay in here.

I take her outside to her little kiddie pool outside my back door and she walks out with me on her own and back in on her own when she is done and that is the only exercise she gets. Other than the occasional getting up to eat and flap her wings.

Can you give me any suggestions of what might help her?

Thank you and I am sorry this is so long but its really hard to explain what is going on with her. I appreciate any help or suggestions you might have.

Sincerely,
Deb Higgins October 31st, 2009

Hi Deb,
I have used Valor and Trauma Life on the duck and the African Grey.
I feel both would be appropriate for your duck. I would probably use one drop of each on her head and I would give her a few dried Ningxia Red berries every day if she were mine.

This is just a suggestion but I've known them to be very helpful. I can give you more info later...I had some friends that worked with a lot of birds and I'll have to see if I can find their info..

Healthy Wishes, Sara
November 2nd, 2009

Hi Sara,

I just wanted to send you a follow up on my little call duck Missy. She is doing soooo much better. At first she didn't want anything to do with the Ningxia Berries so I put them aside for awhile. I got them out again about a month ago and she is now addicted to them. She is so funny, she will actually stand in the kitchen by the counter where she knows I keep them and quack until I give her a few. But at first she really started perking up after I used the trauma life on her.. Before she would just sit under the spiral stairs and not get any exercise unless I made her go swimming and she would walk back to her spot under the stairs. Now I never know where I will find her because she has several favorite spots. She follows us around the house now.

When my grandson comes over she gets all excited when he sits on the living room floor and plays with his Legos. She will run over and help him, she loves them and she reaches in the bucket and picks one at a time up and puts them on the floor next to him.

She is a totally different duck now. The only problem I have now is, I think she forgot she is a duck because she could care less about swimming. I have to literally make her stay in the water long enough to get wet, lol.

She does still have the problem going on with her neck sometimes but before she didn't walk very well and now she runs. I don't think I will ever be able to put her with the others but at least she is getting around and doing a lot better. I'd say 90% better.

Sorry this is so long but I wanted to give you an update and thank you for the excellent advise.

Have a great day, Sincerely,
Deb Higgins

P.S. Another quick story about Missy. At Christmas time we had a party and there were unfamiliar people in and out of here. Every time a person she didn't know came through the door, she quacked up a storm and went running over to check them out. Ummmm, do you think that she thinks she's a dog?

Dog & Cat Emergency Bucket

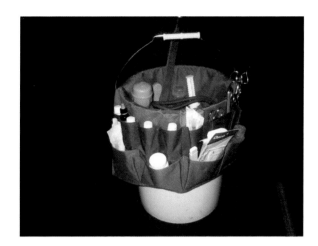

Scissors

Gauze

Leather Gloves: a traumatized animal may bite

Tweezers, Pliers: removing porcupine quills

Medical Clamps: object removal

Vet Wrap

Dog Toenail Clippers

Leash and Muzzle

Small and Medium Syringes

Bottle of Distilled Water

Small Stainless Steel Dish: for mixing oils

Animal Scents Ointment

Essentialzyme: digestive enzymes

Copaiba: anti-inflammatory, pain, stomach distress

Peppermint: stomach upset, pain, car sickness

Ginger: car sickness, pain

DiGize: bloat and stomach upset

Thieves: trips to the vet, shows, etc

Thieves Household Cleaner: cleaner

R.C.: breathing

Peace and Calming: high stress

Purification: wound cleansing, bug bites

Melrose: open wounds

Lavender: wound cleansing, tissue regeneration

Helicrysum: pain, bleeding

Trauma Life: accidents, abuse, neglect

PanAway: pain

Valor: grounding, balancing, aligning skeletal structure

Ortho Sport: pain, arthritis, sore muscle, strain

Olive Oil/ Coconut Oil: diluting

Equine Emergency Bucket

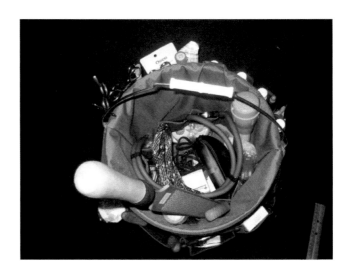

Stethoscope

Gauze

Baster

Vet Wrap

Large Syringe

Small and Medium syringes without needles

Bottle of Distilled Water

Small Stainless Steel Dish

Digital Thermometer/Plastic Covers

Scissors

Tweezers

Medical Clamps

Rasp

Hoof Knife and Hoof Pick

Halter and Lead Rope

Wire Cutters

Animal Scents Ointment

Bottle of Detoxzyme: digestive enzymes, colic

Peppermint: pain, colic, founder

DiGize: digestion, colic

Thieves Spray: foaling umbilical cord, antiviral, antibacterial

Thieves: infection, immune system

Thieves Household Cleaner: cleansing

Longevity: immune system, malignant growths

R.C. : respiratory system

Peace and Calming: relaxation, peace

Melrose: antiseptic, antibacterial, infection

Idaho Balsam Fir: pain and depression

Helicrysum: bleeding, pain

Lavender: wound cleansing, tissue regeneration

PanAway: pain

Valor: bone/joint pain, structural realignment

Copaiba: inflammation, strengthens other oils

Ortho Sport: pain, sprains, wounds

V-6, Coconut or Olive Oil: diluting

The Worksheets

The following three pages are here to help you keep track of the oils that you use during different applications. You will find a list of the many places you may need to apply oils. There is room to make notes about the kind of oil you have used, as well as the number of drops you applied.

I find them to be very helpful for me to keep track of what oils are working on which issues.

Feel free to photo copy them to use on your dogs, cats and/or horses.

**Please do not sell them as your own.

Canine Essential Oil Application/Raindrop Session

Name

_____

Age

_____

Mouth_____
Bridge of Nose _____
Top of Head _____
Neck (front) _____
Neck (back) _____
Left Ear _____
Right Ear _____

Chest _____
R. Forearm _____
L. Forearm _____
R. Carpals _____
L. Carpals _____
R. Foot (pad) _____
L. Foot (pad) _____

Withers _____
Back _____
R. Brisket _____
L. Brisket _____
Belly _____
Loin _____
Tail _____

R. Thigh _____
L. Thigh _____
R. Stifle _____
L. Stifle _____
R. Hock _____
L. Hock_____
R. Foot (pad) _____
L. Foot (pad) _____

Other

_____
_____
_____
_____
_____
_____
_____

Follow up Suggestions

_____
_____
_____
_____
_____
_____
_____

Owner Release:
I have chosen to have my dog(s) receive an Essential Oil Session. I understand the outcome is not guaranteed. I will not hold session administrator(s) responsible in any way for the health of my dog(s).

_____
Owner Signature
Copyright 2011 Sara Kenney, Mindy Schroder
www.saralivingwell.com

Feline Essential Oil Application/Raindrop Session

Ear Nose Neck Back Loin Thigh Withers Chest Brisket Stifle/Knee Forearm Carpals (Wrist) Foot Hock Tail

Name_____

Age_____

What Oils Where

Mouth_____
Bridge of Nose_____
Top of Head_____
Neck (front)_____
Neck (back)_____
Left Ear_____
Right Ear_____

Chest_____
R. Forearm_____
L. Forearm_____
R. Carpals_____
L. Carpals_____
R. Foot (pad)_____
L. Foot (pad)_____

Withers_____
Back_____
R. Brisket_____
L. Brisket_____
Belly_____
Loin_____
Tail_____

R. Thigh_____
L. Thigh_____
R. Stifle_____
L. Stifle_____
R. Hock_____
L. Hock_____
R. Foot (pad)_____
L. Foot (pad)_____

Other_____
_____
_____
_____
_____
_____
_____

Notes

_____
_____
_____
_____
_____
_____
_____
_____
_____
_____
_____
_____
_____
_____

Owner Release:
I have chosen to have my cat(s) receive an
Essential Oil Session. I understand the outcome
is not guaranteed. I will not hold session
administrator(s) responsible in any way for the
health of my cat(s).

Equine Essential Oil Application/Raindrop Session

Name

_____

Age

_____

Tongue _____

Forehead _____

Poll _____

Ears _____

Throat Latch _____

Cheek _____

Chest _____

Crest _____

Neck _____

Withers _____

Shoulder _____

Back/Spine _____

Point of Hip _____

Croup _____

Dock of Tail _____

Barrel _____

Umbilical Area of Belly _____

Mid Belly _____

R. Elbow _____

L. Elbow _____

R. Knee _____

L. Knee _____

R.F. Hoof _____

L.F. Hoof _____

R. Stifle _____

L. Stifle _____

R. Gaskin _____

L. Gaskin _____

R. Hock _____

L. Hock _____

R.H. Hoof _____

L.H. Hoof _____

Other _____

_____

_____

_____

Follow Up Suggestions

_____

_____

_____

_____

Owner Release:

I have chosen to have my horse(s) receive an Essential Oil Session. I understand the outcome is not guaranteed. I will not hold session administrator(s) responsible in any way for the health of my horse(s).

About the Author

I have loved the study of natural health solutions! I read books, did a correspondence course, went to a Holistic Clinic for a month, had fabulous mentors, checked out companies, ordered products, experimented on my family...waited for someone to get sick so I could try something new. BUT it cost a lot of money and had no monetary return...until I was introduced to Young Living Essential Oils.

I tried the oils and got consistent results for all kinds of things. We all became happier and healthier... experimentation never smelled so good!

Because the oils worked so well on myself and my family I, of course, turned to using them on my animals. The results were so wonderful that I had to start sharing what I was learning!

I travel around the United States teaching oiling clinics for horse farms and horse rescues.

Index

Abscesses,Dogs: 18

Abscesses,Cats: 52

Abscesses,Horses: 64

Acupressure: 49

Aggressive,Dogs: 18

Agressive,Cats: 53

Allergies,Dogs: 18

Allergies,Cats: 53

Anal Glands, Dogs: 20

Asthma, Horses: 65

Arthritis, Dogs: 20

Arthritis, Cats: 54

Beestings, Bug Bites, Ticks,Dogs: 21,22

Beestings, Bug Bites, Ticks,Cats: 54

Bleeding,Dogs: 22

Bone Chips,Horses: 77

Botulism, Horses: 66

Calming, Horses: 67

Cancer, Dogs: 23

Cancer, Ovarian Tumor, Melanoma: 77, 78

Cold and Flu, Dogs: 25

Cold and Flu, Horses: 68

Colic, Horses: 69

Depression, Dogs: 25

Depression, Cats: 54

Diarrhea, Dogs: 26

Diarrhea, Cats: 55

Diffusing Oils: 90

Disinfecting, Dogs: 26

Disinfecting, Horses: 71

Ears, Dogs: 27

Ears, Cats: 55

Eyes, Dogs: 29

Emergency Bucket, Dog and Cat: 93

Emergency Bucket, Horse: 94

Falls, Body Trauma, Dogs: 30

Falls, Body Trauma, Horses: 70

Fear, Dogs: 30

Fever, Dogs: 30

Flies, Fly Spray, Horses: 72

Food, Dogs: 19,31

Food, Cats (see also Allergies): 53

Founder, Horses: 73

Grieving, Dogs: 32

Grieving, Cats: 54

Hearing, Dogs: 33

Heart Problems, Dogs: 33

Hoof Infections, Horses: 74

Hip Dysplasia, Dogs: 33

Hyper Bouncy, Dogs: 34

Immune System, Horses: 75

Impaction Constipation, Dogs: 34

Impaction Constipation, Cats: 55

Index

Impaction Colic, Horses: 69

Injury, Dogs: 35

Injury, Cats: 55

Insecurity, Dogs: 35

Kennel Cough, Dogs: 36

Kidneys/Bladder, Dogs: 36

Kidneys/Bladder, Cats (see also, UTI's): 60

Lacerations, Horses: 76

Leg Injuries, Horses: 77

Melanoma, Horses: 77

Nervous Anxiety, Dogs: 37

Odor Control, Dogs: 38

Ovarian Tumor, Horses: 75

Parasites, Dogs: 39

Parasites, Cats: 58

Parvovirus, Dogs: 39

Passing Away, Dogs: 41

Passing Away, Cats: 58

Poisoning, Cats: 59

Porcupine Quills, Dogs: 42

Pregnancy, Dogs: 43

Raindrop Technique: 85

Seizures/Strokes, Dogs: 44

Skin, Horses: 80

Strangles, Horses: 80

Tendons/Ligaments, Dogs: 44

Tendons/Ligaments, Horses: 80

Thyroid, Dogs: 46

Transportation, Horses: 80

Trauma, Horses: 81

Tumors, Dogs: 46

Tumors, Horses: 78

Twisted Gut, Horses: 81

UTI, Cats: 60

Vaccinations, Dogs: 46

Vaccinations, Horses: 76

Vomiting, Dogs: 48

Vomiting, Cats: 61

Wounds, Dogs: 48

Wounds, Cats: 61